SERMON
on the
MOUNT

40 Days of Learning the

Ways of the Kingdom

JEREMY BACON

a renew.org discipling resource

Jeremy Bacon has produced a wonderful exposition of the Sermon on the Mount. In fact, I think it's a model of how biblical exposition ought to be done. On one hand, it's deeply rooted in biblical theology and the original meaning of the text. On the other hand, it is written in a down-to-earth style that sets the meaning of the text in the context of everyday life. As a result, it is loaded with insights that will help you both understand the Sermon on the Mount and live out its message so you can be more like who Christ calls you to be. If you're a disciple of Jesus, you need to read this book.

—**John Whittaker**, adjunct professor of New Testament and creator of *The Listener's Commentary*

Jeremy Bacon is one of the smartest Bible students I know, so his crystal-clear, bite-sized teachings through Matthew 5–7 will bless you. But for me, Jeremy's conversation with his Wiccan coworker, his deliverance at the Red-Bull-and-vodka work party, and his hard-won forgiveness when marriage and ministry punched him hard are the best parts of the book. He hasn't just studied the Sermon on the Mount; he's fought to *live* it. Jeremy has built his house on the rock (Matthew 7:24), and this book can help you do the same.

—**Matt Proctor**, president of Ozark Christian College

It's the most famous sermon in history. Jeremy Bacon provides readers forty topics for forty days with the heart of Jesus. The book integrates exegetical excellence, but it's not a stilted commentary. Filled with poignant illustrations, including candid confessions from the author, it's a down-to-earth conversation that will instruct and inspire you to live the blessed life of a kingdom disciple.

—**Richard A. Knopp**, executive director, RoomForDoubt.com; author of *Truth About God*

Bacon has brilliantly weaved together theology and disciple making with profound practical insights on how Jesus' most famous sermon should be lived out. This incredible resource will challenge any disciple of Jesus to live deeper and fuller in him. This book is a much-needed resource today.

—**Andrew Jit**, founder of MiT Global

I love this book. Jeremy is masterful at combining insightful and delightful with real-world practical. No other book has done more to help me picture how to live out Jesus' Sermon on the Mount.

—**Daniel McCoy**, coauthor, *Real Life Theology Handbook* and *Real Life Theology Conversations*

Contents

1

The Sermon

(Matthew 5–7)

Now when Jesus saw the crowds, he went up on a mountainside and sat down. His disciples came to him, and he began to teach them. He said:

"Blessed are the poor in spirit,
for theirs is the kingdom of heaven.
"Blessed are those who mourn,
for they will be comforted.
"Blessed are the meek,
for they will inherit the earth.
"Blessed are those who hunger and thirst for righteousness,
for they will be filled.
"Blessed are the merciful,
for they will be shown mercy.
"Blessed are the pure in heart,
for they will see God.
"Blessed are the peacemakers,
for they will be called children of God.
"Blessed are those who are persecuted because of righteousness,
for theirs is the kingdom of heaven.

"Blessed are you when people insult you, persecute you and falsely say all kinds of evil against you because of me. Rejoice and be glad, because great is your reward in heaven, for in the same way they persecuted the prophets who were before you.

"You are the salt of the earth. But if the salt loses its saltiness, how can it be made salty again? It is no longer good for anything, except to be thrown out and trampled underfoot.

"You are the light of the world. A town built on a hill cannot be hidden. Neither do people light a lamp and put it under a bowl. Instead they put it on its stand, and it gives light to everyone in the house. In the same way, let your light shine before others, that they may see your good deeds and glorify your Father in heaven.

"Do not think that I have come to abolish the Law or the Prophets; I have not come to abolish them but to fulfill them. For truly I tell you, until heaven and earth disappear, not the smallest letter, not the least stroke of a pen, will by any means disappear from the Law until everything is accomplished. Therefore anyone who sets aside one of the least of these commands and teaches others accordingly will be called least in the kingdom of heaven, but whoever practices and teaches these commands will be called great in the kingdom of heaven. For I tell you that unless your righteousness surpasses that of the Pharisees and the teachers of the law, you will certainly not enter the kingdom of heaven.

"You have heard that it was said to the people long ago, 'You shall not murder, and anyone who murders will be subject to judgment.' But I tell you that anyone who is angry with a brother or sister will be subject to judgment. Again, anyone who says to a brother or sister, 'Raca,' is answerable to the court. And anyone who says, 'You fool!' will be in danger of the fire of hell.

"Therefore, if you are offering your gift at the altar and there remember that your brother or sister has something against you, leave your gift there in front of the altar. First go and be reconciled to them; then come and offer your gift.

"Settle matters quickly with your adversary who is taking you to court. Do it while you are still together on the way, or your adversary may hand you over to the judge, and the judge may hand you over to the officer, and you may be thrown into prison. Truly I tell you, you will not get out until you have paid the last penny.

"You have heard that it was said, 'You shall not commit adultery.' But I tell you that anyone who looks at a woman lustfully has already committed adultery with her in his heart. If your right eye causes you to stumble, gouge it out and throw it away. It is better for you to lose one part of your body than for your whole body to be thrown into hell. And if your right hand causes you to stumble, cut it off and throw it away. It is better for you to lose one part of your body than for your whole body to go into hell.

"It has been said, 'Anyone who divorces his wife must give her a certificate of divorce.' But I tell you that anyone who divorces his wife, except for sexual immorality, makes her the victim of adultery, and anyone who marries a divorced woman commits adultery.

"Again, you have heard that it was said to the people long ago, 'Do not break your oath, but fulfill to the Lord the vows you have made.' But I tell you, do not swear an oath at all: either by heaven, for it is God's throne; or by the earth, for it is his footstool; or by Jerusalem, for it is the city of the Great King. And do not swear by your head, for you cannot make even one hair white or black. All you need to say is simply 'Yes' or 'No'; anything beyond this comes from the evil one.

"You have heard that it was said, 'Eye for eye, and tooth for tooth.' But I tell you, do not resist an evil person. If anyone slaps you on the right cheek, turn to them the other cheek also. And if anyone wants to sue you and take your shirt, hand over your coat as well. If anyone forces you to go one mile, go with them two miles. Give to the one who asks you, and do not turn away from the one who wants to borrow from you.

"You have heard that it was said, 'Love your neighbor and hate your enemy.' But I tell you, love your enemies and pray for those who persecute you, that you may be children of your Father in heaven. He causes his sun to rise on the evil and the good, and sends rain on the righteous and the unrighteous. If you love those who love you, what reward will you get? Are not even the tax collectors doing that? And if you greet only your own people, what are you doing more than others? Do not even pagans do that? Be perfect, therefore, as your heavenly Father is perfect.

"Be careful not to practice your righteousness in front of others to be seen by them. If you do, you will have no reward from your Father in heaven.

"So when you give to the needy, do not announce it with trumpets, as the hypocrites do in the synagogues and on the streets, to be honored by others. Truly I tell you, they have received their reward in full. But when you give to the needy, do not let your left hand know what your right hand is doing, so that your giving may be in secret. Then your Father, who sees what is done in secret, will reward you.

"And when you pray, do not be like the hypocrites, for they love to pray standing in the synagogues and on the street corners to be seen by others. Truly I tell you, they have received their reward in full. But when you pray, go into your room, close the door and pray to your Father, who is unseen. Then your Father, who sees what is done in secret, will reward you. And when you pray, do not keep on babbling like pagans, for they think they will be heard because of their many words. Do not be like them, for your Father knows what you need before you ask him.

"This, then, is how you should pray:

'Our Father in heaven,
hallowed be your name,
your kingdom come,
your will be done,
on earth as it is in heaven.
Give us today our daily bread.
And forgive us our debts,
as we also have forgiven our debtors.
And lead us not into temptation,
but deliver us from the evil one.'

Our Father in heaven, hallowed be your name.

"For if you forgive other people when they sin against you, your heavenly Father will also forgive you. But if you do not forgive others their sins, your Father will not forgive your sins.

"When you fast, do not look somber as the hypocrites do, for they disfigure their faces to show others they are fasting. Truly I tell you, they have received their reward in full. But when you fast, put oil on your head and wash your face, so that it will not be obvious to others that you are fasting, but only to your

Father, who is unseen; and your Father, who sees what is done in secret, will reward you.

"Do not store up for yourselves treasures on earth, where moths and vermin destroy, and where thieves break in and steal. But store up for yourselves treasures in heaven, where moths and vermin do not destroy, and where thieves do not break in and steal. For where your treasure is, there your heart will be also.

"The eye is the lamp of the body. If your eyes are healthy, your whole body will be full of light. But if your eyes are unhealthy, your whole body will be full of darkness. If then the light within you is darkness, how great is that darkness!

"No one can serve two masters. Either you will hate the one and love the other, or you will be devoted to the one and despise the other. You cannot serve both God and money.

"Therefore I tell you, do not worry about your life, what you will eat or drink; or about your body, what you will wear. Is not life more than food, and the body more than clothes? Look at the birds of the air; they do not sow or reap or store away in barns, and yet your heavenly Father feeds them. Are you not much more valuable than they? Can any one of you by worrying add a single hour to your life?

"And why do you worry about clothes? See how the flowers of the field grow. They do not labor or spin. Yet I tell you that not even Solomon in all his splendor was dressed like one of these. If that is how God clothes the grass of the field, which is here today and tomorrow is thrown into the fire, will he not much more clothe you—you of little faith? So do not worry, saying, 'What shall we eat?' or 'What shall we drink?' or 'What shall we wear?' For the pagans run after all these things, and your heavenly Father knows that you need them. But seek first his kingdom and his righteousness, and all these things will be given to you as well. Therefore do not worry about tomorrow, for tomorrow will worry about itself. Each day has enough trouble of its own.

"Do not judge, or you too will be judged. For in the same way you judge others, you will be judged, and with the measure you use, it will be measured to you.

"Why do you look at the speck of sawdust in your brother's eye and pay no attention to the plank in your own eye? How can you say to your brother, 'Let me take the speck out of your eye,' when all the time there is a plank in your own eye? You hypocrite, first take the plank out of your own eye, and then you will see clearly to remove the speck from your brother's eye.

"Do not give dogs what is sacred; do not throw your pearls to pigs. If you do, they may trample them under their feet, and turn and tear you to pieces.

"Ask and it will be given to you; seek and you will find; knock and the door will be opened to you. For everyone who asks receives; the one who seeks finds; and to the one who knocks, the door will be opened.

"Which of you, if your son asks for bread, will give him a stone? Or if he asks for a fish, will give him a snake? If you, then, though you are evil, know how to give good gifts to your children, how much more will your Father in heaven give good gifts to those who ask him! So in everything, do to others what you would have them do to you, for this sums up the Law and the Prophets.

"Enter through the narrow gate. For wide is the gate and broad is the road that leads to destruction, and many enter through it. But small is the gate and narrow the road that leads to life, and only a few find it.

"Watch out for false prophets. They come to you in sheep's clothing, but inwardly they are ferocious wolves. By their fruit you will recognize them. Do people pick grapes from thornbushes, or figs from thistles? Likewise, every good tree bears good fruit, but a bad tree bears bad fruit. A good tree cannot bear bad fruit, and a bad tree cannot bear good fruit. Every tree that does not bear good fruit is cut down and thrown into the fire. Thus, by their fruit you will recognize them.

"Not everyone who says to me, 'Lord, Lord,' will enter the kingdom of heaven, but only the one who does the will of my Father who is in heaven. Many will say to me on that day, 'Lord, Lord, did we not prophesy in your name and in your name drive out demons and in your name perform many miracles?' Then I will tell them plainly, 'I never knew you. Away from me, you evildoers!'

"Therefore everyone who hears these words of mine and puts them into practice is like a wise man who built his house on the rock. The rain came down, the streams rose, and the winds blew and beat against that house; yet it did not fall, because it had its foundation on the rock. But everyone who hears these words of mine and does not put them into practice is like a foolish man who built his house on sand. The rain came down, the streams rose, and the winds blew and beat against that house, and it fell with a great crash."

When Jesus had finished saying these things, the crowds were amazed at his teaching, because he taught as one who had authority, and not as their teachers of the law.

2

Crowds or Disciples?

"Now when Jesus saw the crowds, he went up on a mountainside and sat down. His disciples came to him, and he began to teach them." (Matthew 5:1–2)

The Sermon on the Mount is dangerous.

Maybe that's why we embroider it and put it on our walls: "See, there it is, framed by pretty flowers and happy clouds." Nothing to worry about here. We fall into the trap of thinking that since we know it, we've actually listened to it.

That's where I was when the Sermon on the Mount took hold of me. It started innocuously enough. My plan was to prepare lessons for some Maasai guys in southern Kenya on how to interpret the Bible. I needed a working text, and the Sermon on the Mount seemed the obvious place to go.

My inventory job at a home improvement store doesn't use a whole lot of my brain, so I started memorizing Matthew 5–7 at work. As I walked around with a clipboard doing whatever it is I do, I thought I was preparing lessons for other people. But something else happened as I memorized, meditated on, and dissected the Sermon on the Mount. It was dissecting me. I eventually had the devastating realization that, after growing up as a preacher's kid, getting a bachelor's and master's in theology, and doing a short stint in professional ministry, I had only waded in the shallows.

This sermon blew my worldview apart. Jesus proclaims that, behind the crumbling ground that I walk on and the fading light by which I see, there is something far more real. As Aslan puts it at the end of *The Chronicles of Narnia*, the world we live in every day is nothing but the shadowlands[1]—an opaque, two-dimensional copy of the real thing. It was hard enough to wrap my mind around the truth that this "real thing" is not a metaphor, but a metaphysical reality. It is also a way of living. The patterns of behavior that we develop from our basic drives and from the world around us are also a faded copy of the real thing. Born and steeped in the church for all my forty years, I heard Jesus saying that this faded copy was my life. I had been living in the shadowlands.

I'd like to invite you to have a seat on the grass next to me and see what Jesus has to say to you. I definitely think it's important, but I can't pretend that it's going to be safe.

Hearing what Jesus has to say is also going to take a lot of work. There are exegetical details and questions to sort out. For instance, why focus on the Sermon on the Mount at all? It's not like Matthew 5–7 is somehow "more inspired" than the rest of Scripture—some kind of "canon within the canon." Nevertheless, Matthew intended to present this sermon as something special.

He begins (4:23) and ends (9:34) the larger passage with identical words that summarize what the chapters in between are all about: "Jesus went through _____ , teaching in their synagogues, proclaiming the good news of the kingdom, and healing every disease and sickness." Chapters 8 and 9 show Jesus "healing every disease and sickness." That leaves "teaching in their synagogues," and "proclaiming the good news of the kingdom," which is what chapters 5–7 are meant to flesh out. Of the five major speeches in Matthew, the purpose of this one is to tell us what Jesus' message was.[2]

That's a big deal.

Matthew underscores this with a phrase most English translations leave out. In 5:2, the Greek literally says, *"And opening his mouth,* he taught them, saying . . . " As information, this is redundant. Of course he opened his mouth. That's how you say things. The point is rhetorical. It's a way of saying, "Slow down. Pay attention. What you're about to hear is important."

To determine the significance of the sermon for you, look at the characters in the story. Since we are about to read three straight chapters of Jesus talking, it's easy to forget that this speech happens in a narrative context. The characters are: Jesus, the crowds, and the disciples (5:1–2). If you're looking for whom to identify with, you're not Jesus. He's unique. That leaves the crowds and the disciples. The "disciples" are the ones who have signed on to follow Jesus. The sermon is addressed to them. So, for instance, when Jesus says, "You are the light of the world" (5:14), the "you" applies pretty much the way we've always taken it—to those who follow Jesus. That can include people in the twenty-first century just as it included some of the folks who sat on the hill in front of Jesus. This is probably why the sermon has enjoyed such enduring appeal. It applies directly.

But the "crowds" are also listening. In 5:1, it almost looks like the presence of the crowds is what prompted the sermon in the first place. Yes, Jesus is teaching his disciples, but he wants the crowds to hear. In the Gospels, the "crowds" are the fence-sitters. They don't oppose Jesus, but they haven't made the commitment to follow him, either. We would probably call them "seekers." This means that the makeup of Jesus' audience is much like that of any large church service today—a core group of committed followers and a large number of people who haven't committed but are interested enough to hear more. There has been a lot of hand-wringing over how to reach this kind of audience. In the Sermon on the Mount, we see that Jesus' strategy is to let the "crowds" listen in while he explains to his followers what life in the Kingdom is like.

Against the advice of every marketing consultant, Jesus is not gentle.

He delivers a sermon that is dangerous to both segments of his audience. The disciples heard Jesus' claim of who he is, and they accepted it. This is dangerous because the commitment is not theoretical. They haven't merely assented to a set of propositions. They haven't just signed their names to the roster of some club. The commitment to follow Jesus is a commitment to actual changes in behavior. As James (whose letter echoes this sermon a great deal) says, "Faith by itself, if it is not accompanied by action, is dead" (James 2:17). Look at the number of imperatives in this sermon. There's no getting around the fact that Jesus is telling us to do things.

And the things he's telling us to do are radical. This sermon will challenge you in every way you don't want to be challenged. (If the Pharisees' response to Jesus is any indication, this goes double for people who already consider themselves "religious.") It will shine light on every area of your life that needs to be surrendered to him. The only way to respond to this sermon as a true follower of Christ is to begin turning

This sermon will challenge you in every way.

everything over to him. Everything. The process will be difficult, sometimes painful, and it will last the rest of your life. But there is no partial buy-in. It's all or nothing. Accepting Christ means taking him as your Lord and Master. Is he really the example and guide for your life? Or are you just here for the show?

"Here for the show" describes the crowds—people who, for the time being, remain neutral. Jesus pushes them to something more. He extends comfort to them, but the comfort is in the context of an invitation. He shows them what the Kingdom of God is and tells them that the Kingdom is for them. It's up to them to step off the fence.

But this invitation comes with serious warnings. At some point, intentionally or not, you've chosen your path (7:13–14); you've built your house on something (7:24–27). Yes, there is a natural period of searching and learning before you make this kind of life choice. But that's a halfway house. You can stay a while, but you can't live there forever. The longer you put the choice off, the more disingenuous your indecision becomes. If you never commit, you're not really seeking. You're just playing games.

This sermon is dangerous because it shakes us awake. This world is broken, but we develop so many ways to cope with life that we lose sight of how broken it all is (including us). Jesus' Sermon on the Mount shatters all of our illusions like glass. His stark portrayal of the way things should be lays bare the bankruptcy of the way things are. After reading this, the illusions are gone, and we know we can't stay where we are. We may be reluctant to go forward—it looks like it costs too much. But can we really go back? Can we live in the shadowlands, having seen them for what they really are? Every choice to go back on the fence is a decision to deliberately blind ourselves. Next time, it will be harder to see. A choice to go back establishes a willingness to not respond to Jesus. It will be harder to respond next time. And eventually, time is up. Follow this story to the end, and the "crowds" are no longer fence-sitters. They are the ones calling for Jesus to be crucified (Matthew 27:20–23). This sermon is dangerous because reading it has consequences. It will sift you. You must respond one way or another, and the choice you make will echo into eternity.

That choice was put to me once I saw that I was wading in the shallows. It was clear that I was not okay. Would I respond to the call to go deeper? Or would I try to ignore it and go about my business?

What character was I in this story?

To read this sermon is to be faced with the choice: crowds or disciples? Once you've heard the question, there's no going back.

1. Why do you think Jesus wants the crowds to hear this sermon?

2. What do you think keeps people on the fence when it comes to following Jesus?

3. How did Jesus first get your attention?

4. On a scale of 1 to 10—if 1 is "I'm not interested" and 10 is "I'm all in"—where would you rate yourself right now? Why?

3

Jesus

*"Now when Jesus saw the crowds, he went up on a
mountainside and sat down. His disciples came to him and
he began to teach them. . . . When Jesus had finished saying
these things, the crowds were amazed at his teaching,
because he taught as one who had authority, and not as
their teachers of the law."* (Matthew 5:1–2; 7:28–29)

What is this all about? We can imagine an anonymous man traveling all the way from Syria to see Jesus (Matthew 4:23–25). Surely he was asking this question. Back home, he first heard the stories—there was a man in Galilee teaching some novel things. He normally wouldn't have cared, but some people swore they saw miracles. Something was happening. Once he made it to Galilee, he saw it with his own eyes. A woman was carried to Jesus on a stretcher but walked away on her own two feet. After that, this Syrian man, like other people from up to a hundred miles away, started following Jesus wherever he went. He had to know—what was this? What did it mean? What was it all about?

It's the question on everyone's mind as Jesus sits down to preach. This sermon covers a lot of ground. It's "about" a lot! It might be easy for us to miss that one of the biggest things it is about is the man everyone had traveled to see. This sermon says a lot about Jesus himself.

Jesus' audience didn't miss this. Once the sermon was over, as they walked home processing what they just experienced, their main takeaway had to do with the man himself. The way he spoke implied something about who he was. He spoke with authority (Matthew 7:28–29).

If I have a question about an issue I'm not familiar with, I'm going to seek out an authority on the subject. An "authority" is someone who doesn't need to seek someone else out (which all the rabbis were famous for doing). Because of something about them, their words carry a force of their own.

So who was he? What allowed Jesus to speak like this?

The Sermon on the Mount gives plenty of answers.

Christians today are familiar with the great Christological statements of, say, John—that Jesus is the divine Word made flesh (John 1:1–14). Or maybe Paul's statements that Jesus is "before all things, and in him all things hold together" (Colossians 1:17). In him, "all the fullness of the Deity lives in bodily form" (Colossians 2:9). These statements were written to largely Graeco-Roman audiences. Maybe, since we are children of Western Civilization, these expressions resonate with us because we still have some of that Graeco-Roman thought in our cultural DNA.

Matthew's (and Jesus') audience didn't. Matthew is the most Jewish of all the Gospels. It's so Hebraic in thought and language that some scholars have toyed with the possibility that Matthew actually wrote it in Hebrew. In the Sermon on the Mount, Matthew paints a picture of Jesus using a distinctly Jewish color palette. First, when Jesus walks up a hill and sits down, his disciples come sit at his feet (5:1–2). His body language is using grammar they know well. When a rabbi is ready to teach, he sits. Jesus is clearly presenting himself as a *teacher*.[3]

But that barely scratches the surface. In verse 1 of his Gospel, Matthew introduces Jesus as the *Messiah*—the anointed leader of God's people. The ancient world tended to think collectively. They focused on the group more than the individual. So, in Old Testament thought, there is a sense in which the leader stands in the place of the entire community. He is the people. One place we can see this is in the sin offering. If the high priest (an anointed leader of God's people) sins, he brings guilt on *all the people*, and the required offering is a bull. This is the same offering required if the entire community sins (Leviticus 4:3, 13–14).

It would be intuitive for Matthew's audience that as Messiah, Jesus himself embodies the nation. That's what leaders do. How much more so the Messiah? That's why nearly everything Matthew writes leading up to the Sermon on the Mount shows Jesus recapitulating the history of Israel in his own life. Israel (Jacob) was the miraculous child of a promise; Jesus is the miraculous child of a promise (Matthew 1:18–23). Israel went down to Egypt; Jesus goes down to Egypt (Matthew 2:13–14). Israel came up out of Egypt; Jesus comes up out of Egypt (Matthew 2:15, 19–20). Israel went through the water; Jesus goes through the water (Matthew 3:13–15). Israel went through the wilderness; Jesus goes through the wilderness (Matthew 4:1–11). This probably explains why, if you read the Old Testament passages Matthew quotes, many don't seem to be predicting anything. They're just telling Israel's story. That's the point. Jesus fulfills them because he *is* Israel. But unlike Israel in the Old Testament story, Jesus is doing it right. We see this most clearly in Jesus' time in the wilderness. He is tempted, just as the Israelites were in their wilderness, but where they failed, Jesus stays faithful.

Now picture this: You're a member of Matthew's Jewish audience. The story of Israel is your cultural heritage, and you just read four chapters of Jesus recapitulating that story right up to Israel's time in the wilderness. And then Jesus *walks up a mountain and starts teaching*. There is no way you're not going to think of Moses, Sinai, and the giving of the Law. That's the next part of Israel's story. Many commentators say that Matthew is portraying Jesus as a new Moses. Since Jesus is the fulfillment of *everything* in Israel's story, of course he's the new Moses. But he's so much more.

When Moses goes up the mountain, he's not the one talking. When Jesus goes up the mountain, he is. If the picture in Matthew 5 mirrors Sinai, it's not clear that Jesus is standing in the place of Moses. Yes, Jesus is "the prophet" like Moses who was to come (Deuteronomy 18:18). But the prophets punctuated all their oracles with the signature phrase, "Thus says the Lord." In the Sermon on the Mount, Jesus doesn't say, "Thus says the Lord." His signature phrase is, "But *I* tell you . . ." In this recapitulation of the Sinai story, Jesus is the one at the *top* of the mountain speaking *down*. Jesus is acting as the very voice of God. He *is* the voice from the mountain. John may not have a corner on high Christology when he depicts Jesus as the "Word of God." In a distinctly Hebrew way, Matthew is saying almost exactly the same thing.

Moreover, at the end of his sermon, Jesus talks about "that day" (Matthew 7:21–23). "That day" is prophetic shorthand for "the day of the

Lord." Judgment Day—the great day when God will vindicate his people, settle all accounts, and put things right. And Jesus assumes, without argument or explanation, that on the Great Day of the Lord, he will be the judge.

Teacher, Messiah, Prophet, the very voice of God. One could hardly paint a larger picture of who Jesus is. But we can add one more brush stroke. Parallelism is the defining feature of Hebrew poetry (which much of this sermon is). At the end of the Beatitudes, Jesus blesses those who are persecuted "because of righteousness" (Matthew 5:10). Then in the very next verse he says that his followers are blessed when they are persecuted "because of *me*." Jesus is paralleled with righteousness itself.

One of my professors had several conversations with a local rabbi. Once, he asked the rabbi why he didn't accept Jesus as Messiah. The rabbi said it was because if you take Jesus' words seriously, he is claiming to *be* Torah. That claim would, of course, be absolutely unacceptable.

Unless it's true.

Jesus' audience walked away stunned ("shell-shocked" would be a surprisingly accurate translation), not because they just heard a bunch of pretty words, but because, in those words, in this Word, they just encountered the God of the universe. The key to the Sermon on the Mount is not *what* it's about but *whom* it's about. Because the Sermon on the Mount is, at its core, an invitation into the very heart of God.

The key to the Sermon on the Mount is whom it's about.

THINK ABOUT IT

1. More and more in the modern world, we come into contact with other faiths and other belief systems. While we can often find common ground on different principles, in what way is Jesus presenting himself as different from any other teacher?

2. Why do you think Jesus' audience found his teaching so shocking? Would people find it shocking today for the same reasons or for different reasons?

3. In your faith life so far, what prominence has Jesus himself had? Is he "front and center" in the church activities you engage in, or somewhere on the margins?

4. How could your faith practice focus more on not simply knowing *about* Jesus, but on knowing Jesus himself?

4

Heaven

"Blessed are the poor in spirit, for theirs is the kingdom of heaven." (Matthew 5:3)

The problem with raising kids in the church is that they don't understand that they should accept transcendent mysteries as ineffable, shrug their shoulders, and move on. Kids ask questions. Oh, the discussions I would get into with my kids. I'd be tucking them into bed and BAM!, we're having an in-depth conversation about the nature of the Trinity. I don't know how many times I turned off the light thinking, "I have a master's degree in this, but I feel like I'm driving on a mountain overpass and just barely keeping this thing on the road."

The question we really got stuck on was, "Where is heaven?" We came back to this one over and over. They couldn't shake the idea that heaven is some future disembodied place where you go when you die. Most people can't. That view is not entirely wrong, but it's wrong enough to be a serious problem for understanding the Sermon on the Mount.

In this sermon, Jesus uses forms of the word for "heaven" (noun, adjective, etc.) twenty times in three chapters. If we want to grasp what Jesus is trying to say, believe it or not, "heaven" is probably the most important word to understand.

I found this out by accident when I did a study on every time the Greek word *ouranos* is used in the New Testament. Like any non-technical word, "heaven" can have different shades of meaning. First of all, heaven is where the birds fly (Matthew 6:26). Second, heaven is where the stars are (Hebrews 11:12). Third, heaven is where God is (Matthew 6:9).

This is probably what Paul means when he talks about the "third heaven" (2 Corinthians 12:2–4). Not the place where the birds fly, and not the place where the stars are, but the place where God is. Although folks in the ancient world understood things like outer space differently than we do, they understood that these were three different places. A bird can't fly to where the stars are.

More importantly, the place where God is is not merely farther out than the place where the stars are. No, it is above the "*highest* heavens" (Ephesians 4:10). It is a different kind of place. Seeing this heaven is not just a matter of seeing really far. You have to have the "heavens opened" (Acts 7:56). More than a place, heaven is a layer of reality that has to be revealed.

In 1 Corinthians 15:35–53, Paul pushes the limits of human language to try to express what this reality is like. He parallels the things "of heaven" to the things that are "spiritual," so it would probably be accurate to say that "heaven" refers to the spiritual realm. But the word "spiritual" brings up all the wrong ideas for us. We usually take "spiritual" to mean "immaterial," but Paul is clearly saying that it is not. In fact, it is something far sturdier than anything we experience in this world. Our present body is natural and of the earth. It is characterized by weakness and dishonor. It is perishable and mortal. But the future body is spiritual and of heaven. It is imperishable and immortal. By the time Paul talks about this future body being characterized by strength, it's clear we're not talking about something immaterial. The heavenly/spiritual body is a body that is not less tangible than our present one, but somehow more tangible (cf. 2 Corinthians 5:4).

If words fail, maybe a picture will help. Jesus' resurrected body is a preview of this spiritual body. The context of the whole discussion in 1 Corinthians 15 is Paul arguing that we know we will be resurrected because Jesus was resurrected. As part of his argument, he explains that we will be resurrected in the same form in which Jesus was resurrected. "Just as we have borne the image of the earthly man, so shall we bear the image of the heavenly man" (1 Corinthians 15:49). First Corinthians 15:35–53 is Paul's attempt to explain what that form is like. Jesus is "the firstfruits of those who have fallen asleep" (1 Corinthians 15:20). The first day's harvest isn't fundamentally different than the second day's. Rather, it lets us know exactly what's coming. So, as John says, "We know that when Christ appears, we shall be like him" (1 John 3:2).

So what was Jesus' resurrected body like? On the one hand, it was clearly a material body. To reassure his disciples of this, Jesus ate some fish right in front of them (Luke 24:37–43). On the other hand, he was able to walk through the locked door of the upper room (John 20:19).[4] Here's the thing: Jesus wasn't able to walk through the door because his body was some ethereal, ephemeral thing. No, he was able to walk through the door because, compared to his resurrected body, *the door was the ethereal, ephemeral thing.* This world is weak and passing away. Look out your window. Everything you see—the sky, the trees, the ground, and whatever we put on it—is a wisp of smoke. It may look solid, but it is decaying and passing away (Isaiah 51:6). It is a mere shadow (Hebrews 8:4–5). Heaven, the "spiritual" realm, is the real thing. So we'll equate "heaven" with "the spiritual realm," understanding that it is more solid and enduring than this one (Matthew 6:19–20).

This heaven is the place where God is, and it is also where he rules. As the Lord's Prayer implies, his will is done there (Matthew 6:10). So it is where his "Kingdom" is. The phrases "the Kingdom of Heaven" and "the Kingdom of God" are always synonymous (Matthew 19:23–24). Perhaps Matthew uses "Kingdom of Heaven" (often just "heaven") most often because he wants us to remember the nature of this realm. In this sense, "heaven" (i.e., the Kingdom of Heaven) is the spiritual realm where God rules and everything is the way it should be.

The story of Scripture is the story of God working to make things right. In that story, it is from heaven that God intervenes in this broken world. Although heaven is not literally "up," the metaphor of "heaven is up" is so intuitive that God himself uses it. His voice comes from heaven (John 12:28), he sends bread from heaven (John 6:31), and sometimes he sends fire from heaven (Luke 17:29).

God's ultimate intervention "from heaven" was sending Jesus himself. In fact, Jesus' favorite designation for himself in the Gospel of John is "the one sent." Where was he sent from? Heaven (John 6:38). And in the work of Christ, the Kingdom of Heaven itself is breaking in. The Kingdom is a present reality.

God's ultimate intervention "from heaven" was sending Jesus himself.

It has "come near" (Matthew 3:2; 4:17; 10:7). All of Jesus' miracles are the Kingdom of God breaking in to make things right (Luke 11:20). They preview what that Kingdom is like (things aren't broken there), and they evidence that the Kingdom is near.

Yet the Kingdom is not fully here. The world is still broken. We pray that God's will might be done on earth (Matthew 6:10) because it all too often isn't. As the theologians say, the Kingdom is "now, but not yet." It is a present reality awaiting future fulfillment. In chapter 13, when Matthew gives Jesus' parables of the Kingdom, so many of the parables play off of this idea of a present reality awaiting future fulfillment. In the Kingdom, the good seed has been planted. It's a present reality. But it's going to be mixed with weeds until the end (Matthew 13:24–30). A lot of the parables talk about seeds, and what is a seed but a present reality awaiting future fulfillment?

The final fulfillment comes when Jesus returns. At the end of the story, all things are made new. Then the holy city, Jerusalem itself, the dwelling place of God, is what comes down from heaven (Revelation 21:1–2). Heaven is the place where God is, and the place where God is comes down to his people. "Look! God's dwelling place is now among the people, and he will dwell with them" (Revelation 21:3). So, ultimately, Jesus isn't taking us to heaven. He's bringing heaven to us. It will be a "new heaven and new earth." It will be different from the old one, not because it's not material, but because it's not broken (Revelation 21:4). When my kids ask me what heaven will be like, I say, "Look around you. It's this, but not broken anymore."

This is the story of Scripture: a broken world that God is preparing to make new. It is the story of the coming of the Kingdom of Heaven. This Kingdom is the focus of the Sermon on the Mount—from the first beatitude (5:3) to Jesus' final warnings (7:21)—so we have to understand what it is:

The Kingdom of Heaven is the spiritual realm
(which is actually more solid and enduring than this one)
where God is, where God rules, and where everything is as it should be.
In Christ, this Kingdom is a present reality awaiting future fulfillment.

Where is heaven? According to Matthew, it is "near." Peel back the layer of this shadow world, and it's right there—real, close, and accessible. The implications for how I live the next time I walk out the door are enormous. It upends every investment I make here and indicates that true value lies in totally different things. To borrow Tony Campolo's metaphor,[5] what does it mean to start switching the price tags back from what I thought was valuable to what is truly valuable? How do I relate to things? To time? To myself? To God? To other people in the vast array of contexts in which I encounter them? It's hard to process. It changes everything. If I acknowledge that the Kingdom has come near, how should I live?

The Sermon on the Mount is Jesus' answer to that question.

THINK ABOUT IT

1. In the past, how have you thought of heaven? What images did the word conjure up for you?

2. What do we miss if we only think of heaven as "the place you go when you die"?

3. What does it mean that the Kingdom has "come near"? How does this relate to the Kingdom being "now, but not yet"?

4. What do Jesus' miracles show about God's heart for this broken world?

5

Kingdom Blessing

"Blessed are the poor in spirit, for theirs is the kingdom of heaven." (Matthew 5:3)

I n a superhero show I watched years ago, the token reporter was interviewing the supervillain, who presented himself as a famous and successful businessman. People thought he was just an ordinary rich guy known for hostile takeovers. Wanting to understand what made him tick, the reporter asked, "What do you want?" His answer, sincere and insightful, was, "Happiness."

Isn't that what we're all looking for? Heck, we Americans have "the pursuit of happiness" enshrined in one of our founding documents. But finding happiness is the trick. Unlike supervillains, most people don't think that melting cities with a space laser will make them happy, but we're not sure what will. We're like my youngest son, who thought he would find happiness in the experience of riding a bicycle with no hands and his eyes closed. He did not. (Don't worry. His adult teeth grew in just fine.)

So Jesus hits a nerve by beginning the Sermon on the Mount with happiness—"beatitude" in Latin. Most English translations of Matthew 5:3–12 use the word "blessed" because we English speakers can't agree on what the concept of "happiness" even is. For Jesus' audience, it would have been a full-bodied sense of overall well-being.

But let's not forget the context here. Having walked up the side of a mountain to start teaching, Jesus already has his audience thinking about the covenant God made with Israel at Sinai. Jesus' "blessings" are clearly playing off of the "blessings and curses" that cap off the old covenant (Leviticus 26 and Deuteronomy 28). But Jesus' blessings have two major differences.

First, *who* is blessed, or rather, what qualifies a person for blessing, is different. In the old covenant, note that the blessings come at the end. We get to them after all the rules. And so the only real qualification given for blessing is, "Did you follow the rules?" "If you fully obey the LORD your God and carefully follow all his commands I give you today, the LORD your God will set you high above all the nations on earth. All these blessings will come on you and accompany you if you obey the LORD your God" (Deuteronomy 28:1–2).

Jesus' blessings, however, can't refer back to any set of rules because *he hasn't said anything yet.* Jesus starts with the blessings. It's literally the first word out of his mouth. The implication is that Jesus' system isn't about rules. There are no imperatives in the Beatitudes (unless you count "rejoice and be glad" in Matthew 5:12). Like any part of Scripture, we can mine the Beatitudes for principles for living, but Jesus never actually says, "Be this." (The fact that "Beatitudes" sounds like "be-attitudes" is just an unfortunate accident of English.) Jesus is not a Greek logician laying out necessary and sufficient conditions for blessing. He's a Hebrew rabbi painting a picture—sketching a portrait of a citizen of the Kingdom of God. The qualifying question in Jesus' blessings is not, "Do you check off every box on this list?" but, "Do you see a resemblance in this picture?" If you do, the Kingdom is for you.

Jesus' system isn't about rules.

The remarkable thing is how accessible this portrait is. Yes, some of the characteristics are traits we should foster (like being merciful or being peacemakers) or aspire to (like being pure of heart), but the first few have nothing to do with anything we do or are. They are states of affairs that we find ourselves in (being poor of spirit or grieving). The first people in line for blessing are those who bring absolutely nothing to the table. This is a portrait that any of us (if we're honest with ourselves) can find ourselves in.

The second difference between Jesus' blessings and the blessings of the old covenant is the content of the blessings. In Leviticus and Deuteronomy, the rewards are practical, material provision, like rain, crops, and military security. The Beatitudes go far beyond that. First, we get comfort for all we've suffered (5:4) and all the material provision and security we need (5:5). After that, we get to be the people we truly want to be (5:6). Then the rewards turn outward as we find mercy in spite of all the damage we've done to God's creation (not least of all ourselves) (5:7). Reconciled to God, we can see his face (5:8), and, as we become agents of reconciliation, the family resemblance between us and God becomes clear (5:9). In searching for fulfillment, what more could we possibly look for?

Yet we are looking. We're looking hard. A lot of people look for happiness in the easiest places—artificially produced "happiness" buzzes around every corner. They look in the bottom of a bottle or in the rest of that doughnut. In the next episode on their streaming service or the next video on the porn site. In the next drug spike or the next gadget that's "as seen on TV." But these all have diminishing returns. To get the same buzz next time, they have to go bigger. Some people spend their entire lives chasing that dragon, only to find that it's taken everything and given nothing.

Other people try "happiness idols" (money, pleasure, power, and fame)[6] that are less obviously destructive. But happiness studies (a surprisingly young branch of psychology/social science) have confirmed ancient wisdom. These are all dead ends.

One of the clearly positive findings in happiness studies is that truly growth-promoting happiness is found in healthy, close relationships. Jesus is not surprised. Fostering healthy relationships (i.e., "peacemaking") caps off the Beatitudes. In fact, once Jesus gets into the meat of this sermon, healthy relationships are the first thing on the agenda (5:21–32). Healthy relationships are included in the Kingdom package.

But healthy relationships are not so easy to come by. I've had to watch some of my friends and coworkers run to find happiness in another person's arms, only to end up in a slow-moving train wreck that lasted years. Truly healthy relationships require people who are growing into healthier individuals. But growth is hard. A lot of impressive stuff is coming out of the "personal development" crowd, and the clearest thinkers are realistic about the commitment that growth requires. Like physical exercise, personal growth requires pushing ourselves at the very points where we are weak. We have to deliberately step into behavior that we know is going to hurt. This takes dedication, discipline, and even sacrifice. I was stunned to hear some personal development leaders acknowledge that this kind of dedication can't be generated internally. It's just too hard. Once the going gets tough, you only find sufficient motivation for personal growth when you believe that you are part of something bigger than yourself. This provides meaning and purpose that outweigh the pain and sacrifice of growth. In other words, happiness is founded on being part of something bigger.

But not just anything. Let's face it, violent radicals believe they are part of something bigger than themselves, but they don't tend to score high on the "happiness" scale. What you are a part of matters. And some people spend their whole lives trying to find what will actually fit the bill. But this presents a dilemma. If we try to figure out and design this "something bigger" on our own, even if a bunch of us work at it together, at the end of the day it's not really bigger. It's just an idol. It's our image that we tried to scale up. To be truly bigger than us, it has to come from outside of us.

All of us.

Maybe it's not so crazy to believe that it has to be proclaimed to us from a voice on top of a mountain. What if all this striving we see in the world, all this grasping for happiness, is what it looks like when people are desperately searching for the Kingdom of God but have no idea that's what they're looking for? They want that pearl of great price. They're willing to give everything for it. It's just not in any of the places they're looking. But what if Jesus got their attention? What if he got them to stop, sit down on a hill, and listen? What if, as he spoke about the reign of God, they realized that the blessing they were seeking *is* the Kingdom of Heaven? That this Messiah is offering the very thing their hearts have always been searching for, and they don't have to search anymore?

It has found them.

1. What ways have you seen people pursue happiness that didn't get them there? What ways did?

2. When you hear people summarize the message of Christianity, what problem is it supposed to solve? What does it change to think of Christianity as presenting "the happiness (the overall well-being) that we're all really looking for"?

3. What do you want?

4. Do any of the Beatitudes themselves already resonate with you? Which ones? In what way?

6

Poor in Spirit

"Blessed are the poor in spirit, for theirs is the kingdom of heaven." (Matthew 5:3)

During college, I spent a summer in England traveling around helping various churches. The couple who led a very small church north of London often just needed someone to watch their seven-year-old daughter and one-year-old son so they could have a breather. They were good kids, but I didn't have much experience.

I was feeding the one-year-old one day when he got the hiccups. Problem. This precious, pasty little British boy couldn't eat if he kept hiccupping it all back out. Worse, he might choke on it. So I dug into my repertoire for how to cure the hiccups and learned that yelling, "Boo!" at a one-year-old is not an effective solution. He cried, the hiccups remained, and it took a couple days for him to start trusting me again.

That summer gave me a lot of time to think about why Jesus says that the Kingdom belongs to little children (Matthew 19:14). When we preach this, we often point to positive characteristics that are common among kids. But if we're honest, they're not universal. So why would Jesus say this? What is something that is true of all kids? I found an answer that summer—all kids cry.

A lot.

When children cry, they are saying three things: (1) "I have a problem," (2) "I can't solve it," and (ideally) (3) "You can." The younger we are, the more we clearly understand that we have problems we can't solve. As we get older, we still have plenty of these problems, but we get better at masking and ignoring them. That makes it hard for us to be poor in spirit.

There's a fair amount of confusion over what it means to be "poor in spirit." It looks like Luke has the original formulation of this beatitude—"blessed are the poor" (Luke 6:20)—which Matthew "spiritualizes." But what does "spiritualizing" even mean? We tend to assume it means that Matthew took a concrete state (being poor) and, by adding "of spirit," turned it into a pious, other-worldly virtue. This may be what *we* mean by "spiritualizing" something, but it's not how any New Testament author uses the word "spirit."

Paul, for instance, usually uses "spirit" to talk about things that pertain to the Holy Spirit (as in gifts "of the Spirit" [1 Corinthians 12:1]). In this sense, Paul certainly doesn't want us to be poor in the spirit. He wants us to be filled with the Spirit (Ephesians 5:18)! Other times, Paul uses "spirit" to point to the spiritual realm in general (1 Corinthians 15:46). But we saw in Chapter 4 that when Matthew talks about the spiritual realm, he talks about the things "of heaven." In this sermon (Matthew 6:20), Jesus is going to insist that we *not* be poor in the things of heaven!

Remember that Matthew is steeped in Hebrew thought. To understand his language, instead of looking forward to the later New Testament, we need to look backward to the language of the Old Testament. In the Psalms, a person's "spirit" refers to their inner life in general: "I remembered you God, and I groaned, I meditated, and my *spirit* grew faint" (Psalm 77:3). To be "poor" is to lack resources, so a person who is "poor in spirit" lacks the inner resources to cope with the circumstances they are facing.

The exact phrase "poor in spirit" is never used in the Psalms, but several authors of various psalms fit the description. Their circumstances include dealing with people who seek to harm them (Psalms 142, 143), suffering physical illness (possibly Psalm 77:1–12, but definitely Psalm 6), or agonizing over the depth of the damage their sin has done to their relationship with God (Psalm 51:7–17). These authors all express trouble in their "spirit." "When my spirit grows faint within me, it is you who watch over my way," writes one psalmist. "Listen to my cry, for I am in desperate need" (Psalm 142:3, 6). That word "desperate" seems to capture well the sense of being poor in spirit. We could also add "overwhelmed," the NASB translation for "grows faint." This gives us a good working description: *to be "poor in spirit" is to be overwhelmed and desperate.*

> To be "poor in spirit" is to be overwhelmed and desperate.

Of course, literal, physical poverty is one thing that can lead a person to be overwhelmed and desperate. Since Luke's "poor" are "hungry" and they "weep now" (Luke 6:20–21), they seem to fit the bill. This means that Matthew is not "spiritualizing" Luke. Rather, Luke's "poor" are, in fact, a sub-category of Matthew's "poor in spirit." They are poor in spirit as a result of being straight-up poor.

Being "poor in spirit" is a visceral, emotional experience. Think of a time when life was "just too much." Whether it was your kids or your job or your health or a relationship, or it was the year the pandemic started and *everything* was crashing down. That's being poor in spirit. The poor in spirit are on the wrong side of a meltdown.

We can identify two essential components of being "poor in spirit." The first is an awareness that *things are bad*. This is usually an immediate, "on the ground" awareness. But sometimes it comes from a more general grasp of the brokenness of the world. Non-Christian thinkers—philosophers, religious leaders, think-tank types—often have profound insight into what's wrong with where we are. They know we can't stay here. They know we need a better place. Such folks sometimes reason themselves to the very doorstep of the Kingdom of God, but ideas can only get you to the doorstep. It takes power to get inside. Only Jesus has that power. He is the door (John 10:9; Matthew 11:27–28). These unbelievers lack the second element of being poor in spirit. Beyond seeing what's wrong with where we are, we have to see our utter inability to get where we need to be. The poor in spirit are desperate not only because they know *things are bad* but also because they know *they are powerless*.

Tragically, many Christians who have access to this power have only a dim awareness of what's wrong with where they are. Maybe that's because, in much of the Western world, we have the bottom layers of Maslow's hierarchy of needs (basic physical needs and security) pretty well taken care of. The idea that we need to *get out now* seems a little nutty. Instead we can leisurely pursue things like esteem needs or self-actualization, or maybe just chill where we are. Someone once said that it's like we're living in a cardboard box, not realizing that our cardboard box is in the middle of a cathedral. Instead of looking for a way to get out, we're using a set of markers to scribble pictures on the inside of our box to make it look a little nicer.

Of course, no one's life is perfect. Things will go wrong. But, in our mostly comfortable situation, problems are not taken as a sign of fundamental brokenness. They're just a sign that some government official hasn't done their job very well. The solution isn't radical; we just need to get someone else in there who can do things right. This world may be a fixer-upper, but, all the same, it's home.

Ironically, believers who live this kind of life also find themselves on the doorstep of the Kingdom. Even though they have the power to get in, they have no sense of urgency, so they aren't even trying. This is why, in Luke, Jesus adds, "Woe to you who are rich, for you have already received your comfort" (Luke 6:24–25). The rich aren't looking for a way out. They have this cardboard box fixed up pretty well, thank you. This makes their situation all the more dire. They've made their home on the Titanic. The ship is taking on water, but they're fluffing the pillows and polishing the floorboards. They're numb to the reality that they *need to go!*

In their desperation, the poor in spirit don't have either of these problems. They know that *things are bad.* This world has failed them. They look around and know that the ship is sinking. For heaven's sake, they're already waist-deep in water! And they know *they are powerless.* If help doesn't come from the outside, that's it. They're done.

The desperation of the poor in spirit has severed their tether to the things of this world, and Jesus is ready to catch them. "The righteous cry out, and the LORD hears them; he delivers them from all their troubles. The LORD is close to the brokenhearted and saves those who are crushed in spirit" (Psalm 34:17–18).

Why are the poor in spirit blessed? Because they have no illusions of finding what they need in this world. They are ready for the Kingdom.

1. What kind of God would put the poor in spirit first?

2. What are some problems we like to think we can solve, but probably can't? Why? What problems do we just ignore?

3. Have you ever thought you were in a great place in life, and then realized you weren't? What was that like?

4. Have you ever found God when you were in an overwhelming or desperate situation?

7

Mourn

*"Blessed are those who mourn, for they
will be comforted."* (Matthew 5:4)

Sitting in the basement of a monastery trying to make a meaningful connection with a dozen total strangers was an awkward experience. It was a "community building workshop" based on M. Scott Peck's *The Different Drum.*[7] We sat on folding chairs in a circle, and one of the few guidelines we were given was, "Speak only when you are moved to speak."

Most of us ended up sharing the pain we were experiencing. A young lady in college realized she'd chosen the wrong field. An experienced professional struggled to get a charter school going. Two ladies were there because their vision for starting a ministry in their area was floundering. One man's divorce stirred up criminal charges, and he couldn't see his son. The room was full of broken relationships and dying dreams.

Eventually, one person's discomfort boiled over (which is actually part of the process), and she complained, "If we're going to share, why does it have to be all this heavy stuff about our suffering?" Another lady answered with an observation, "Suffering is a universal part of the human experience. No matter how diverse we may be, we can always relate on the level of suffering. We all speak that language."

At least one major religion—Buddhism—takes suffering as its starting point. Indeed, any system of thought that doesn't address suffering will quickly become irrelevant. A system that doesn't talk about suffering isn't talking about my life.

So it's no surprise then that suffering makes an early appearance in the Sermon on the Mount: "Blessed are those who mourn, for they will be comforted" (Matthew 5:4). At one time, it may have preached well to say that this "mourning" specifically refers to sorrow over our sin. The word certainly can be used that way (James 4:8–9), but that meaning comes from the context, not from the word itself. The word Jesus uses (*pentheo*) does not focus on any particular reason for our grief. It's also not the word for outward expressions of grief (like crying, etc.; see Acts 21:13). It refers to the emotion itself. It's the emotion you feel when mourning a death (Mark 16:10) or facing a devastating loss (Isaiah 3:26). Jesus is simply saying, "Blessed are those who feel deep, painful loss."

In a perfect world, this wouldn't make any sense. Grief and happiness are opposites. But this world isn't perfect. We *will* suffer. We can deny it or hide from it, but that's not going to get us to happiness. The only hope for a sense of well-being is to have a way to deal with suffering—to overcome it.

Scholars often wrestle with suffering as a logical problem. They talk about "the problem of evil"—the most extreme end of the suffering spectrum. In the simplest terms, the problem of evil is that *that which should not be, is.* In religious terms, if God is all good and all powerful, why is there evil? Put technically, are these three statements—(1) God is maximally good, (2) God is maximally powerful, (3) evil states of affairs obtain—logically coherent? Can all three be true?

You might be surprised to learn that Alvin Plantinga solved this problem (in *God, Freedom, and Evil*,[8] and summarized several other places). To recap his argument, free will is the key (as we, the mere mortals on the ground, tend to suspect). It is possible that all evil states of affairs result from free-will decisions, and it is possible that free will is a good that outweighs the cost. So a powerful God who allows evil as the cost of free will could still be good.

Done.

Plantinga's achievement is monumental, but why didn't it make the news? Why isn't this common knowledge shouted from the housetops? The dirty secret about the intellectual problem of evil is that even if you solve it, nobody cares. If a parent shares Plantinga's answer with their child who has cerebral palsy, it rings hollow. You see, we don't want to know why God allows evil things *in general*. We want to know why God allowed the specific thing *I* am suffering. This "Why?" we cry out is not an intellectual question; it is an emotional one. God understands that an intellectual answer will never land. It's almost beside the point. That is why, even though God is asked the question at least four times in Scripture (Job; Jeremiah 12; Habakkuk; Luke 13), he never answers it. Usually he says, "I hate to tell you this, but things are going to get a lot worse." At most, he says, "You just have to trust me."

As an emotional question, the only answer to the problem of evil is the grief process itself. People have to grieve. In the face of suffering, the only way to get through to an emotionally better place is to mourn. People need to be in denial, to try and bargain out of their loss, to be angry, to be depressed. The best thing we can do for them is to grieve with them (Romans 12:15). That's the one thing Job's friends did right (Job 2:11–13). When we are suffering loss, it helps to know that we're not alone.

That's exactly what Jesus did. He stepped down into our suffering and grieved with us (John 11:35). In the cross, Jesus walked the road of suffering all the way to the end. This means that, no matter where we find ourselves stepping onto that path, we find Jesus. He's already there, waiting for us, ready to walk with us as far as we need to go.

But that is not God's only answer to the problem of suffering. God spends no time dealing with evil as an intellectual problem. He takes on evil as a practical problem. His goal is not to explain evil. His goal is to end it.

When Jesus died on the cross, he took the curse. Every curse—from the curse of the law (Galatians 3:13) to the very curse of Adam (Romans 5:17). In the story of Scripture, our sin and the brokenness of the world are intertwined (Genesis 3:17–19). On the cross, Jesus took it all. And on the cross, it died with him. He was raised as the firstborn of a new creation (Revelation 1:5). In his resurrection, death is swallowed up in victory (1 Corinthians 15:54–55). No matter how immediate our suffering may feel, the resurrection stands as a testimony that the suffering we grieve is not the last word.

The suffering we grieve is not the last word.

The Holy Spirit—poured out from the ascension of Christ—is how God's emotional and practical answers to suffering connect with us. Living in us, the Holy Spirit is the presence of God to comfort us—we are not alone (John 14:16–18). Also, through the work of the Holy Spirit, we are part of the new creation (Romans 8:10; 2 Corinthians 5:17). The Holy Spirit living in us is a down payment (2 Corinthians 1:22), foreshadowing a world where we won't suffer anymore (Revelation 21:4).

When I'm suffering right now, I'm not going to be happy about it. I'm going to be in denial; I'm going to be angry; I'm going to be depressed. But when I cry, I know, first, that I'm not crying alone. I am crying in the arms of Jesus. And, second, I know a day is coming when I won't be crying anymore. The crucifixion, resurrection, and ascension of Jesus Christ is God's answer to the problem of evil. That is his comfort for those who mourn.

THINK ABOUT IT

1. In the Western world, we have a hard time dealing with grief—especially with recognizing that people often grieve for a very long time. Why do you think that is?

2. Has anyone come to you when you were grieving and said something that did not help? What was it?

3. Have you brought your grief to Jesus in the past? What happened?

4. Satan often speaks corrosive messages—about us and about God—in our times of grief. How do the cross, resurrection, and ascension answer those messages?

8

Meek

"Blessed are the meek, for they will inherit the earth." (Matthew 5:5)

n fifth grade, I was on a community-league soccer team. When the season was over, I was awarded "Most-Improved Player," which means I was terrible. The only goal I ever scored was for the other team. Our coach was great, though. The night before game day, he would have us over to his house for a carb-filled spaghetti dinner. He cared about relationships, and respect was his top priority. When we won the "Best Sportsmanship" award at the regional tournament, he was probably happier than if we had gotten first place.

For the regular season, we tied the first and last game. We won all the rest.

Then he moved, and we had a different coach the next year. We were having a scrimmage one practice. I was on defense, and I knocked over one of the guys who was going for our goal. I said, "Sorry," as I helped him up, but the new coach came over and barked at me, "Don't apologize to him! He's the competition!" That practice was the end of my soccer career.

What does it take to win? In the second century, the Roman emperor Hadrian coined the saying, "Peace through strength." It's been popular ever since. George Washington used it; so did Alexander Hamilton and Ronald Reagan. It has been included in every Republican platform since 1980. It seems like common sense, doesn't it? Be the biggest, baddest person on the block, and you get what you want.

So the idea that the meek will inherit the earth (Matthew 5:5) may sound like the most ridiculous thing Jesus ever said. Understanding what "meek" means doesn't help. It actually makes it worse. To unpack why, we need to figure out who the "meek" are. Looking at a couple of characters can help us with that.

The first is an ancient, poor Israelite. The Hebrew language had several words for the social class of the "poor." This social class was specifically the landless poor in a culture where land was a huge deal. The ancient worldview made a strong connection between a particular land and the people on it. That land was part of their identity. This worldview also saw a strong connection between a god and his land, so land was a connection to the divine. For an Israelite, land was at least a sign of divine blessing. But in a culture where people made a living herding cattle or through subsistence farming, land also meant life. This is partly why an entire book of the Bible is dedicated to the story of Israel inheriting the promised land. Without land, people are undone. They are powerless and vulnerable to exploitation (cf. Psalm 37:14).

The word Jesus uses for "meek" is sometimes used in the Greek translation of the Old Testament for a couple of those Hebrew words for "the poor." But it's only used this way about twenty percent of the time. It's not an exact fit. "The meek" is not a *name* for our landless, poor Israelite, but it describes him well. Since Jesus talks about the meek inheriting the *land* (the word usually translated "earth"), he probably has at least one eye on this guy (Psalm 37:11–14).

Next to this powerless, poor Israelite, we can stand the Greek's ideal ruler. In Greek thought, meekness was not an unfortunate life situation. It was a virtue. You didn't want a king who was apathetic—who had no emotional energy to get anything done. But you also didn't want a king who flew off the handle. Aristotle's happy medium was "meekness." In contemporary terms, you might say that the ideal (meek) ruler is proactive, not reactive. But the virtue of meekness also has to do with how you relate to people. It means "gentle," the opposite of "violent" and "quarrelsome" (1 Timothy 3:3).

This idea of meekness as a virtue appears in Zechariah's description of the Messiah. "See, your king comes to you, righteous and victorious, lowly ["meek"] and riding on a donkey, on a colt, the foal of a donkey"

(Zechariah 9:9). Isaiah doesn't use the word, but he clearly also sees the Messiah as gentle: "He will not shout or cry out, or raise his voice in the streets. A bruised reed he will not break, and a smoldering wick he will not snuff out" (Isaiah 42:2-3; cf. Isaiah 53). Later in Matthew, Jesus will use this word to describe himself (Matthew 11:29), and Matthew will directly quote the verse from Zechariah (Matthew 21:5).

Matthew seems to have an eye on both our poor Israelite and our virtuous Greek king. In interpreting Matthew 5:5, we don't have a clear case for choosing one over the other. Perhaps instead we should look for what these two guys have in common.

Looking at the Greek king, we can affirm what nearly every sermon on this beatitude says: "Meek is not weak." There's nothing weak or passive about that guy! And yet, if we look at our Israelite, meekness obviously doesn't *rule out* weakness. The most we can confidently say is that weakness is not necessary for meekness, but they aren't mutually exclusive, either. If people are weak, they may be meek just because they don't have any other choice.

If meekness isn't necessarily passive, our Israelite shows that it definitely isn't aggressive. It seems easiest to define meekness (and gentleness) by what it is not. *The meek do not dominate and control others.* This description of meekness fits the few New Testament examples we have—submissive wives (1 Peter 3:1–4) and patient teachers (Galatians 6:1; 2 Timothy 2:25). These folks are trying to influence others, but not in an imposing way. As the Greeks put it, meekness is the gentle way you automatically relate to friends as opposed to the harsh way you relate to enemies. Meekness is treating people with dignity and respect rather than trying to dominate and control them. If, like our Israelite, people are meek by default (because they're too powerless to be otherwise), Jesus says, "Don't worry about it. You're blessed." If they have power like our Greek king, but choose not to dominate and control, Jesus says, "Good job choosing the blessed path."

Those who refuse to dominate and control others end up on top.

If the meek inherit the earth, then Jesus is saying that those who refuse to dominate and control others are the ones who end up on top. That's our culture's cue to spit out its drink in shocked incredulity. How could anyone say that with a straight face? Haven't you heard about "red tooth and claw"? It's just science. Only the strong survive. Ours is the age of hostile takeovers, of high-powered consultants, of propaganda, of memes using words as weapons to move opinion where you want it to go. "Will to power," baby! In the real world, the meek get crushed like bugs.

Or do they? Perhaps we're playing fast and loose with our worldview. Even from an evolutionary framework, couldn't a community based on cooperation rather than domination actually be more likely to thrive? Helping each other, rather than eating each other, could be a strength. Our combative culture seems to be choosing, not a truly Darwinian framework, but a Nietzschean/Machiavellian one. This is more of a "will to power" and "win at all costs" strategy. The problem here is that you can compete in a zero-sum game so fiercely that you devastate the landscape. The arena in which we're all trying to live collapses. Everyone loses. As Steven Covey argues, the "dog-eat-dog" worldview is actually the fantasy. In the *real* real world, "win-win" solutions (which require understanding and dignifying the other) are almost always the best long-term solutions.[9]

We need to re-evaluate our business model. Leadership voices from Dale Carnegie[10] to current Christian business consultants stress that treating people with dignity and respect gets measurably better results. How we treat people matters. This is not just an ethical or psychological truth: it's a practical one. A de-escalation training manual for police officers puts so much stress on respect as a tactical move that it states in bold print, "Respect saves lives."[11] There is on-the-ground wisdom to the statement that the meek inherit the earth. Dignity and respect create friends who are assets. Dominance and control create enemies who are obstacles. Meekness really is the best practical approach.

So Christians need to take a long, hard look at the way we've interacted with our culture. If the meek really do inherit the earth, then the minute we start treating people as opponents who need to be defeated, we've already lost (cf. 1 Peter 3:15–16). To what extent have we been drawn into the zero-sum, "us vs. them" game? The problem is not that Christians should never be involved in politics. The problem is that politics in America these days are shockingly toxic. Our public discourse is consumed with little other than demonizing the other side and strategizing their defeat. If Christians want to step into that mess with any integrity, they must be peacemakers, not partisans. If we abandon meekness to accomplish our goals, we not only forfeit our goals, but we walk away from the life Christ has called us to.

We need to follow our Master's example. A guy hanging on a cross isn't forcing anyone to do anything. And yet, this is the event that changed the world.

Meekness is scary. Refusing to try to dominate and control requires trust. Trust in people, yes, but even more trust in God. In Matthew 5:5, Jesus doesn't say that meekness is the most effective way to reach our goals. An inheritance isn't something we achieve. It's something we receive. Being meek means treating people the way Jesus would treat them and then trusting that, whether in this life or the next, God will give us our inheritance.

THINK ABOUT IT

1. Where do you see people prioritizing winning over respecting others?

2. Do you identify more with the poor Israelite or the Greek ruler—do you see yourself as more likely to push or be pushed?

3. People have lots of ways of trying to use force to get their way. Aggression is obvious. Passive-aggressive behavior is not. But they both aim at the same thing—control. Have you ever tried to dominate and/ or control someone? How did that affect the relationship?

4. How could you treat "adversaries" (potential or actual) in your life with respect?

Righteousness

"Blessed are those who hunger and thirst for
righteousness, for they will be filled." (Matthew 5:6)

The doctrine of justification by faith may be killing us.

My sister's church got a new pastor. This church never was her franchise of choice, but they didn't make a big deal about their doctrinal distinctives. They weren't ashamed of them, but they kept them mostly in the background. The focus was on loving Jesus and following him.

That all changed with the new guy. Suddenly, their doctrinal distinctives were front-and-center every week. There was an overwhelming emphasis on our inability to do anything on our own to respond to God. Now, there might be a healthy way to emphasize this, but that's not what was happening. Sensing something toxic in the air, people started leaving. The church's discipleship program disappeared entirely. Somehow, "grace" and "faith" were stifling the desire to pursue Christ.

Before you get out the matches and kindling, I'm not saying that the doctrine of justification by faith is wrong. I'm saying that "justification" is complicated. In his highly recommended book *Justification*, N. T. Wright points out "the tendency for words, like bright three-year-olds, not to sit where you told them to, but to wander around the room, start fiddling with things they weren't supposed to touch, form new relationships . . . and generally enjoy themselves at the expense of the exegete who is trying to keep them under control."[12] When Jesus says, "Blessed are those who hunger and thirst for righteousness, for they will be filled" (Matthew 5:6), the word he uses for "righteousness" is another form of the word we often translate "justification." But it's possible that it is in one chair when Jesus uses it, but has wandered off somewhere else when Paul picks it up to say that we are "justified through faith" (Romans 5:1). We need to explore this possibility because understanding what Jesus means is a matter of life and death. Whatever this "righteousness" is, Jesus pictures the blessed hungering and thirsting after it. A deer doesn't thirst for water because it's curious. It thirsts for water because its life depends on it.

In Romans 5:1, Paul is summing up a three-chapter discussion in which he is clearly thinking of "justification" in terms of the courtroom (see, for instance, Romans 2:1–3). In this picture, God is the judge, and we are the defendants hoping to be acquitted. Here, "justified" is a status that we are hoping the judge grants us. With all the subtlety of a bullhorn, Paul points out that this status does not match our actual behavior. It is an act of grace on the judge's part that looks not at our behavior, but at our faith. In this sense, we could say that "justified" is the status of "acceptable to God" that is granted apart from anything we do.

But look at what happens if we think we've nailed "justification" onto that chair and it can't mean anything else. When Jesus talks about hungering and thirsting for righteousness/justification, he would mean that we are longing for the status of "acceptable to God." It would be heresy to say that we can achieve this status based on what we do. It must be granted by the gracious judge. So "hungering and thirsting for righteousness" would be synonymous with longing to be given grace. To keep from falling into the error of thinking we can ever be "good enough," all the focus is taken off of what we do entirely.

Which is pretty awkward since the rest of the Sermon on the Mount is Jesus telling us a bunch of stuff we are supposed to do. In fact, this sermon clearly raises the bar on our standard of behavior. What's the point of all these instructions if, in this one beatitude, Jesus says that none of it really matters?

This should be our cue to stop the car and check the map. We may have taken a wrong turn somewhere. Instead, Protestant theology sometimes plows ahead, concluding that the Sermon on the Mount sets the bar so high that it's impossible—that the impossibility, in fact, is the point. Since we're saved by grace, you can't be "good enough," and it's misguided to try.

But if the point of the Sermon on the Mount is that it's impossible, why does Jesus fill three chapters with ethical teachings we can't actually follow? Jesus is pretty good with words. If he wanted to say, "You can't be good enough," I don't think he would need three chapters to do it.

We need to step back and let Jesus be Jesus and let Paul be Paul. Of course, the two don't contradict each other, but that doesn't mean they're having the same conversation, either. In the early chapters of Romans, Paul is hashing out a theology of how we acquire a right standing with God. In the Sermon on the Mount, Jesus is painting a picture of what life in the Kingdom looks like. Here, the word "righteousness" is concerned with a different piece of the puzzle.

Outside the courtroom context we looked at earlier, "righteousness" can refer to the *actual conduct* appropriate to a person who is in right standing with God. For instance, "Noah was a righteous man, blameless among the people of his time, and he walked faithfully with God" (Genesis 6:9). Jesus clearly has this practical, lived-out righteousness in mind. In the Sermon on the Mount, righteousness is not some abstract status. It is literally something people do (Matthew 6:1). Since people might be persecuted for it (Matthew 5:10), it's obviously something people can see. It's also something some people can do better than others (Matthew 5:20). In fact, the "surpassing" righteousness of Matthew 5:20 is the summary phrase for the entire body of the Sermon on the Mount. What does this righteousness look like? All the stuff Jesus says to do in the rest of the sermon! Jesus is saying, "Blessed are those who desperately desire to live out this Kingdom life."

> **Blessed are those who desperately desire to live out this Kingdom life.**

Jesus is not talking about how we get into the Kingdom. He's talking about what life in the Kingdom is like. If we say that the point of Jesus' ethical instructions is that they are impossible, we're saying that this way of living which is the Kingdom (Matthew 6:33), which is life, is a pipe dream. We're standing on a road designed by the Almighty to take us exactly where we want to go, and we're putting up barricades with signs saying, "Danger: Do not enter!" Or, as Jesus puts it:

> Woe to you, teachers of the law and Pharisees, you hypocrites!
> You shut the door of the kingdom of heaven in people's faces. You
> yourselves do not enter, nor will you let those enter who are trying to.
> Woe to you, teachers of the law and Pharisees, you hypocrites! You
> travel over land and sea to win a single convert, and when you have
> succeeded, you make them twice as much a child of hell as you are.
> (Matthew 23:13–15)

If we want a Christianity that has no power to transform, let's spend all our time telling the church that admission is free but never flesh out what we're being admitted to. As Peter puts it, we are "redeemed from the empty way of life handed down to you from your ancestors" (1 Peter 1:18). We cannot be saved from one way of life without being brought into a different way of life (Romans 6:15–18). This righteousness the Sermon on the Mount describes is not the way *to* life, it *is* life. To walk in it is to crave life. Not to walk in it is to settle for death.

This perspective does not condemn us to some kind of legalistic perfectionism. Even in this beatitude, we see that Jesus does not expect perfection. In fact, Jesus manages, in only one verse, to embrace every piece of the whole "justification" puzzle. In Matthew 5:6:

1. *There is a standard for living*—Jesus' use of the word "righteousness."
2. *We don't meet that standard.* People "hunger and thirst" for what they don't have.
3. *We are accepted despite not meeting that standard.* We are "blessed" in the state of hungering and thirsting but not actually having.
4. *Yet we have an internal desire for the standard.* We crave it, sensing that it is life. If we don't have it, nothing else matters.
5. *The promise is that we will attain it.* Our desire for righteousness will "be filled"!
6. *This is not something we accomplish by our own strength of effort.* "They will *be* filled" is in the passive voice. All we do is desire it.

If we can lay off junk food long enough, our bodies start to reset and crave food that is healthy. There is a similar spiritual feedback loop. The more we follow Jesus, the more we instinctively crave the life we find there.

Yet the rest of the New Testament stresses that this life is not something we produce—it flows through us as we abide in Christ (John 15:5). This life is the fruit the Holy Spirit produces in us (Galatians 5:22–25). The purpose of all the instructions in the Sermon on the Mount is to reveal blockages—places where we need to surrender and let the life of Christ through. The Sermon on the Mount hints at this when Jesus parallels himself to the very righteousness we've been discussing (Matthew 5:10–11). He is the life we crave. Those who hunger and thirst for righteousness understand that they only truly live when the life of Christ flows through them.

He is life, and we are filled when we are filled by him.

THINK ABOUT IT

1. Have you heard the idea that the point of the Sermon on the Mount is that Jesus' way of living is impossible? If so, did this affect your desire to pursue holiness? Why or why not?

2. Beyond being accepted by God, why would someone crave living well?

3. Looking back at the six "pieces" of the righteousness "puzzle" in this beatitude, which do you find most compelling right now?

4. How can you pursue living Jesus' way, not to earn your way to him, but to let him live through you?

10

Mercy

"Blessed are the merciful, for they will be shown mercy." (Matthew 5:7)

W e do not live in the age of mercy. We live in the age of mob vengeance. Jon Ronson tells the story of a woman who was going on a flight across the Atlantic.[13] While waiting for a connecting flight, she tweeted a tongue-in-cheek joke for her 170 followers. Then she turned off her phone, got on the plane, and fell asleep.

By the time the plane landed, her life had been completely destroyed. Someone with a very large following saw her tweet, did not take it as tongue-in-cheek (but as straightforward and highly offensive), and made her famous. In subsequent days, she lost her job. Her employer couldn't afford to be associated with her. Under the barrage of rape threats and condemnation, she began to lose her own sense of who she was. The mob decided that she was guilty, and they did not have mercy.

Reality TV conditions us to see reality as entertainment. The news teaches us to quickly identify the good guys and bad guys. Disembodied interactions on the internet make us stop seeing people as people. They are memes or faceless comments. Put all that together, and we have a culture in which reality is a video game, and our entertainment is to hunt down and destroy all the "bad guys." Highest score wins. Gotta catch 'em all.

So Jesus is an enormous buzzkill when he says, "Blessed are the merciful, for they shall receive mercy" (Matthew 5:7). We need to see just how far away from mercy this culture of personal destruction has taken us.

The New Testament concept of mercy has three movements: First, we perceive that someone is in a bad spot. Second, we feel compassion for them. And third, we do something to help. Mercy is a compassionate response to the suffering of another person. All three movements are essential, but the emphasis is usually on the last one—the thing we do to help. For instance, the blind guys cry out to Jesus, "Have mercy on us, Son of David!" (Matthew 9:27). Yes, they want Jesus to see their suffering and feel compassion for them, but they especially want him to do something to help (see also Matthew 15:22; 17:15; and 20:30–31). So it's not surprising that the Greek word for a benevolent gift (*eleemosune*—Matthew 6:2) is derived from the word for mercy (*eleos*). A benevolent gift is something we do out of compassion to help someone who is suffering.

Mercy is closely associated with *forgiveness* because forgiveness can be the thing we do to help. We see all the elements of mercy clearly in the parable of the unmerciful servant. The first servant owes the master so much that he and his entire family will be sold into slavery as payment. "At this, the servant fell on his knees before him. 'Be patient with me,' he begged, 'and I will pay back everything.'" So the master sees that the servant is in a bad spot. As a result, "The servant's master took *pity* [or *had compassion*] on him, canceled the debt and let him go" (Matthew 18:26–27). But then the first servant takes a second servant who owed him a little bit of money, beats him up, and throws him into debtor's prison. "Then the master called the [first] servant in. 'You wicked servant,' he said, 'I canceled all that debt of yours because you begged me to. Shouldn't you have had mercy on your fellow servant just as I had on you?'" (Matthew 18:32–33). The lesson? "This is how my heavenly Father will treat each of you unless you forgive your brother or sister from your heart" (Matthew 18:35). In this parable, "mercy" is compassion responding in forgiveness.

Forgiveness is a huge theme throughout Matthew. In fact, Matthew 5:7 closely mirrors Jesus' comments about forgiveness in and around the Lord's Prayer—forgive, and you will be forgiven (Matthew 6:12, 14–15). So, when Jesus says, "Blessed are the merciful, for they will be shown mercy," it's a safe bet that forgiveness is the specific form of mercy he's thinking of.

But forgiveness as mercy has a serious wrinkle. Forgiveness necessarily means that someone has wronged us, and the natural emotional response to being wronged is anger. That's normal. It's instinctive and almost unavoidable.

But mercy necessarily involves compassion, and compassion is also natural and instinctive. In the parable, we are impressed that the master forgave such a large debt, but we also get where he's coming from. Compassion is rooted in empathy, and our brains are hard-wired for empathy. Heather Heyer was struck by a car while protesting the "Unite the Right" rally in Charlottesville. The lady on the scene who cried out, "Medic!" was, in fact, one of the Neo-Nazis.[14] It's not that this lady had a conversion experience. (She found her way back to her Neo-Nazi mindset.) It's that, in that moment, her fundamental wiring won out. She instinctively saw Heather not as an enemy, but as a fellow human being who desperately needed help. She had compassion.

It's pretty hard for a normal person to override empathy. We either have to prime ourselves for it, or, in the moment, we have to choose to override it. Mercy as forgiveness presents us with exactly that choice. When we see the one who has wronged us suffering, empathy is sparking compassion, but the wrong done is triggering anger. I don't think I've ever felt compassion and anger toward the same person at the same time. I'm not sure it's possible. So there is a moment of genuine choice: we can focus on the wrong, or we can focus on the person. We can either let our anger go and feel compassion for them, or we can hold on to our anger and harden our heart. In the face of incompatible impulses, we must choose.

Unforgiveness, then, is a deliberate choice. That's probably why Jesus takes it so seriously. The Sermon on the Mount will give us plenty of time to talk about forgiveness proper. In keeping with the positive tone of this beatitude, let's ask the positive question—how can we keep our hearts inclined toward mercy? If mercy is a response to compassion, and compassion is rooted in empathy, then the key is to keep our culture and the trials of life from blunting our empathy.

How can we keep our hearts inclined toward mercy?

The easiest way to avoid empathy is to essentialize people. Instead of letting them be full-bodied, complicated human beings, we reduce them to some specific, unacceptable feature and see this negative quality as their *essence*. This is who they are. Up close, this can simply mean focusing on how they did us wrong. If it's someone we've never met, it's easy to reduce them to one unacceptable internet post. For good measure, instead of relating to them as individuals, we can relate to them as members of a group: they're one of "those" people, and you know what those people are like.

If you want to be a person primed for mercy, adamantly refuse to essentialize. This can be especially hard these days since there are so many people who seem eager to essentialize themselves. Maybe it's people who insist that they are defined by some particular "identity." Or maybe it's folks who morph political positions into something more like commitment to a cult. They define themselves by a characteristic or group. But a person does not have the ultimate say as to what defines them. Jesus does. What matters is not how they see themselves, but how Christ sees them (1 Corinthians 4:3–4). To him, they are complicated, messy individuals created in God's image and worth dying for.

This has nothing to do with excusing or ignoring anyone's behavior. Mercy doesn't mean viewing people as innocent. It means viewing them as human. This is, after all, exactly what Jesus did for us. He became "fully human in every way" (Hebrews 2:17). The eternal Word took on our common humanity. And, as Hebrews argues, by standing in our shoes, he is able to "empathize with our weakness" (Hebrews 4:15). Empathy, rooted in a recognition of our common humanity, results in compassion. So Jesus became one of us. And the result is that we "receive mercy and find grace to help us in our time of need" (Hebrews 4:15–16). He became like us so that we could become like him. In him, we become people of mercy.

1. What are some instances in Jesus' ministry when he displayed mercy?

2. Have you ever seen "justice" carried out in a way that seemed overboard—where a little more mercy seemed appropriate? Why do you think the ones who carried out this "justice" thought their harsh response was appropriate?

3. Have you ever realized that you were treating someone in an unmerciful way? What did you do when you realized this?

4. In what situations do you tend to feel less empathy—not really acknowledging the common humanity in other people? What could you do to remind yourself of their humanity?

11

Pure in Heart

"Blessed are the pure in heart, for they
will see God." (Matthew 5:8)

n Matthew 15:21–28, Jesus is traveling north of Israelite territory near Tyre and Sidon. When a Canaanite woman with a demonized daughter approaches him to beg for help, he initially ignores her. Even after his disciples pressure him (because she's being so insistent), Jesus is dismissive: "I was sent only to the lost sheep of Israel. . . . It is not right to take the children's bread and toss it to the dogs." But the woman replies, "Even the dogs eat the crumbs that fall from their master's table." Matthew completes the story, "Then Jesus said to her, 'Woman, you have great faith! Your request is granted.' And her daughter was healed at that moment."

It's a nice story, but don't miss the fact that Matthew places it immediately after a heated discussion between Jesus and the Pharisees over what it means to be "clean" (Matthew 5:1–20). This woman whom Jesus is eventually impressed with fails the traditional "clean" test on almost every level. She is a woman, a Gentile (a Canaanite, no less), and has a demonized daughter, for Pete's sake!

I mention this because "pure in heart" is a terrible translation of Matthew 5:8. Jesus uses the technical word for "clean" in this verse. In Jesus' day, there were very few concepts as theologically and even politically charged as being "clean." The Pharisees evolved during the intertestamental period as a group meticulously obsessed with being clean—starting with the regulations in Leviticus and building from there. Unfortunately, the focus tended to be external.

In all fairness, cleanness in the Old Testament is surrounded by external ceremonies which are prompted mostly by external situations—like skin diseases or gross things coming out of someone's body. Let's be honest—the external is easier to focus on. We can evaluate it almost instantly.

But in responding to the Canaanite woman, Jesus emphatically rejects an external definition of "clean." In his ministry, Jesus declares war on superficiality. "Blind Pharisee! First clean the inside of the cup and dish, and then the outside also will be clean" (Matthew 23:26). The conclusion of the discussion in 15:1–20 is that "what goes into someone's mouth does not defile them, but what comes out of their mouth, that is what defiles them" (15:11) because "the things that come out of a person's mouth come from the heart" (15:18). Jesus heals the Canaanite woman's daughter because he sees the woman's internal faith (15:21–28). The establishment-shattering turn that Jesus makes in his ministry is that he's not concerned about outward cleanness. He's concerned about cleanness of the heart.

This theme saturates the Sermon on the Mount. For most of chapter 5, Jesus exposes the ways people try to keep the letter of the law while totally missing its heart. In the first half of chapter 6, Jesus argues that a purely performative religion has no lasting significance. For the rest of chapter 6, he shows that our concern for physical things reveals a heart that is off-center. Even in wrapping up the sermon in chapter 7, Jesus warns that an inside that is not transformed will eventually work its way out. At every step, the heart is what matters. Without that, the rest is pointless.

At every step, the heart is what matters.

Modern English readers mostly get the idea of "the heart," but the biblical concept is far richer than the English one. Yes, it includes our feelings (Genesis 6:6). But it also includes the entire subterranean world of motivations that is usually inaccessible to us (Jeremiah 17:9). It's tempting to call it the "subconscious," but the Biblical concept of "the heart" does not map well onto contemporary psychological models. It's not that one or the other is wrong. They're just looking at things so differently that you can't fit one over the other. For instance, the biblical concept of "the heart" also includes our ability to deliberate and make choices (Genesis 27:41)—our choices being the most conscious of our prefrontal cortex activities. "The heart" can refer to almost any part of our inner life, or to the entire thing as a whole (Psalm 73:26). It can be a way of talking about our self, as deep as it goes. So it's close to an Eastern concept of the "core self" or "essential self."

That, says Jesus, is what needs to be clean.

So I'm toast. I look at my past, and I am well aware of ways I have defiled my heart. And the more Jesus opens his mouth, the worse it gets. Like the ancient Israelite who committed the "unintentional sin" (Leviticus 4:1), I "become aware" (Leviticus 5:5; 4:27–28) of levels of uncleanness that weren't even on my radar. That's painful. It's hard to own up to the violence I have done to my own heart. (If I'm a Pharisee, and my very identity is based on being ceremonially clean, it may be *too* much. Rather than face the reality of my heart, it may be easier to make Jesus stop talking.)

The extent of heart damage is a problem, but so is the depth. If the heart is unsearchable, any attempt of mine to clean it will fall short. I'll just be fooling myself. Without realizing it, I'll be plastering over deeper layers that my devious inner mind doesn't want to deal with. A clean heart? How is that even possible?

Let's ask that ancient Israelite from Leviticus. Leviticus says an awful lot about becoming clean. Take, for instance, people who recover from a skin disease and then bring a guilt offering to become ritually "clean."

First, the guilt offering requires confession (Leviticus 5:5). The person must acknowledge and own up to their sin.

Next, even in some of the simpler cases, they must literally wash themselves and put on clean clothes (Leviticus 15:5–8). In the case of a skin disease, they also have to shave their entire body (Leviticus 14:8–9). That's a little weird, especially for people who are very proud of their beards. They end up smooth like a baby. What do you do with a newborn baby? Wash it and put on fresh clothes. The idea may not be spelled out in words, but the picture is pretty clear.

This person is being born again.

That may be why Jesus seemed so surprised that being "born again" was a new concept to a scholar like Nicodemus. Anyone at the temple constantly saw people who shaved themselves bald, washed, and put on fresh clothes in order to become "clean." How did he miss that?

Next, the person being cleansed is sprinkled in the blood of the sacrifice (Leviticus 14:6–7, 14). Cleansing requires forgiveness (Leviticus 4:31).

Lastly, they are anointed with oil (Leviticus 14:15–18).

Or, as Peter summarizes it for his Jewish audience who had just become aware of *their* sin, "Repent and be baptized, every one of you, in the name of Jesus Christ for the forgiveness of your sins. And you will receive the gift of the Holy Spirit" (Acts 2:38). In the face of unimaginable sin, Peter tells them how to make their heart clean: confess, experience the washing of rebirth, find forgiveness in the blood of the Lamb, and let the anointing of the Holy Spirit do a new work of creation in you.

In Christ, our heart is clean because the Holy Spirit makes it entirely new. As Ezekiel prophesied, God puts his Spirit in us, and this gives us a new heart (Ezekiel 36:26–27). God does a new work of creation in us (2 Corinthians 4:6) making us a new creation: "The old has gone, the new has come" (2 Corinthians 5:17). And this new heart, sprinkled by the blood of the Lamb, is clean (Hebrews 10:22).

But what is the point of becoming clean? Is it just for the sake of being clean—so we can feel better about ourselves? Is it so we can be good boys and girls? To be sure, if you make the tree good, it will bear good fruit (Matthew 7:17–18). Good fruit and a healthy self-image may be features and benefits of Christianity, but they are not the purpose. The goal of the Old Testament sacrificial system was fellowship with God. That which is holy cannot come into contact with that which is unclean. But we have a holy God who wants to dwell with his people (Leviticus 15:31).

The capstone of all the sacrifices is the fellowship offering. Whenever all the sacrifices are offered, this is always the last one. And, in the climax of the fellowship offering, part of the sacrifice becomes a feast that the worshipers symbolically share with God himself (Leviticus 7:16). This is the goal of atonement—to be in the presence of God. This is why David asks for a clean heart. "Do not cast me from your presence," he says (Psalm 51:10–11). A heart that is set right recognizes that this is the only thing that really matters.

In this beatitude, all of life melts away. There is no status, no career, no possessions, no endless ways of passing the time. There is only a person, at the core of their being, standing before their God. In the Old Testament, seeing God was unimaginable. Ritual cleansing can only get us so close. But the promise of the new covenant is that it reaches to the depths of who we are and literally, metaphysically makes us new. Now, with our hearts clean, we don't see the external or the internal.

Because we see him.

THINK ABOUT IT

1. What are some ways we tend to focus on people's exterior instead of their inner character?

2. Have you ever recognized that your heart was in a much worse place than you thought? What was that like?

3. I was baptized when I was nine. As a teenager, I was talking with a friend about what we felt like coming up out of the water. The word we landed on was "clean." Have you had that experience of feeling that you had been cleansed by Jesus? Describe it.

4. How can we rest on the cleanness Jesus accomplished for us—letting his cleanness be our cleanness?

12

Peacemakers

"Blessed are the peacemakers, for they will be called children of God." (Matthew 5:9)

One of the greatest regrets of my life is that I didn't sit off to the side to watch and learn from that lady working the airport desk. Growing up, I never experienced conflict as something resolvable. A person could exit a conflict (by physically leaving) or win a conflict (by the other person backing down and giving in), but I don't think I could have even processed the idea of *resolving* a conflict.

So, traveling home from college on Christmas break, I was mesmerized by the lady working at the airport. Our connecting flight had been canceled. Everyone on that plane had to reschedule for the next day and spend the night in a strange city (and lose a day of Christmas break with whomever they were going to visit). The average temperature in that line was "irate." This woman was catching it in almost every way imaginable. But she never cracked. One by one, she calmly dealt with each traveler. In sorting out their solution, she never broke her civility. Heck, she never stopped being chipper and friendly. It was 11:00 at night, and she was smiling. She was a wizard.

That is not the norm. "It is not good for man to be alone" (Genesis 2:18), but when we get together, we sure can make an awful mess. The first man born on this planet murdered the second one. We're bad at this. But then Jesus comes along and says, "Blessed are the peacemakers, for they will be called children of God" (Matthew 5:9).

The word "peace" calls back to the Hebrew idea of *shalom*, which means overall well-being. It applies to much more than interpersonal conflict, but interpersonal conflict has a really good way of messing up our sense of overall well-being. So the idea of *"making* peace" usually means resolving conflict between two parties. God says of wandering Israel, "Let them make peace with me" (Isaiah 27:5). On the other hand, the second horseman of the apocalypse is given the ability to *take* peace, so people start killing each other (Revelation 6:4).

You are a peacemaker if you reconcile parties that are in conflict. Maybe you're one of the parties, maybe not. It works either way.

> **You are a peacemaker if you reconcile parties that are in conflict.**

Peacemakers are "children of God" because God cares passionately about peacemaking. God's peacemaking is the major theme of Ephesians: God makes peace between himself and humanity (chapter 1), peace between Jew and Gentile (chapters 2–3), peace among believers (chapter 4), and peace in the home (chapters 5–6). If we are to be like God, we will be peacemakers.

Making peace, though, is scary. It's scary because we are broken. We are broken because we have adapted to a broken world. Making peace means stepping into conflict. And conflict triggers the unconscious parts of our brain concerned with survival. Raise the heart rate just a bit, and the emotional brain takes over. By comparison, the problem-solving brain is super slow, so the emotional brain says, "Step aside. We don't have time for you. I've got this."

But it doesn't have this.

The emotional brain has all kinds of maladaptive processes that may get us out alive, but they surely don't produce *shalom*. What's worse is that the emotional brain can talk. Words come out of our mouths. These words may even sound like a rational argument, but if we look at the house our problem-solving brain lives in, the lights aren't even on.

This chapter can't be a full manual on conflict resolution, but we can look at some *preliminaries*—things we need to take care of in ourselves to start taking the posture of a peacemaker. Work on these, and we'll have a good foundation to start learning about making peace.

To have any hope of making peace, we must learn to de-escalate ourselves. Calm down the emotional brain, and let your problem-solving brain take charge. The things our emotional brain tells us are compelling (after all, they sure feel right!). But they're stupid. What the emotional brain wants does not make for *shalom*.

This doesn't mean you should turn the emotional brain off. Good luck responding in a human way without your emotional radar. The emotional brain just can't be in charge. In fact, our problem-solving brain may decide that one of the following strategies is right. But our emotional brain often defaults to them for all the wrong reasons, and things go sideways.

First, the emotional brain often wants to plaster over conflict rather than try to resolve it.

To the emotional brain, being alone is death. Being in a group feels safe. The emotional brain knows what has kept the group intact so far, so doing anything new or off-script (including something that may actually solve the problem) is terrifying. Even if the group itself is terrible—like an abusive relationship or a family with an alcoholic dad. The emotional brain knows how to "keep the peace."

In less threatening situations, our emotional brain still says, "Don't rock the boat." It will settle for what M. Scott Peck calls "pseudo-community."[15] Put on a happy face, pretend everything is fine, and for heaven's sake don't acknowledge anything that might not be. But that means that the underlying issues causing the conflict are still there. They are zombies—burying them doesn't kill them. They'll be back. And, over time, they will probably get worse. So, as Ultron would say, this emotional brain tactic may get us some *quiet*, but it won't get us peace.

Second, if the emotional brain does engage in conflict, it wants to win. When's the last time you saw an action movie that climaxed with a big diplomatic breakthrough? Not what we instinctively want. We want the Michael-Bay punch to the face. We want the Chris-Rock mic drop. Boom! Deal with that! We want to prove a point. The emotional brain finds this very satisfying.

But it's completely useless.

The person we're in conflict with is also in their emotional brain. Their problem-solving brain isn't there to sign for any deliveries. They also want to win. So aiming to win just makes it a zero-sum game that everyone is sure to lose.

The idea of a "decisive win" in an interpersonal conflict is a scam that our emotional brains are selling us. We're trying to impress an audience that is entirely in our head. We're so concerned with what this imaginary audience thinks that we're not listening. Active listening is really our only chance at de-escalating the other person so we can look for ways that we can both win. This is pretty much the opposite of what the emotional brain wants, so we have to actively ignore that zinger our emotional brain is trying to put together.

Lastly, the emotional brain wants to draw a line between "us" and "them." The emotional brain is concerned with the group. For the sake of maintaining the group, there are certain things we just don't do. But if we decide that the person we are in conflict with is not part of "our" group, then the gloves are off. In his mind-blowing book *Conflict Communication*, Rory Miller calls this "othering."[16] (It's a version of the "essentializing" we talked about in connection with mercy.) Whether it's a spat at the grocery store or an all-out war between nations, we come up with a way to view them as "less than." For our emotional brain, this justifies anything we decide to do. And our decisions will be totally unconcerned with peace.

None of this is like God. God in no way minimizes or ignores the rift between us and him. And instead of focusing on "winning," Jesus went to the cross. On that cross, he broke down all dividing walls between "us" and "them" (Galatians 3:28).

Do we want to be peacemakers? Like Paul in his letters, we need to know when not to shy away from conflict. But like Phinehas, we need to take the time to listen and not just charge in to win (Joshua 22). And we need to remember that, in the very covenant that set the Israelites apart, God commanded them not to treat the foreigner among them differently because they had been in the foreigner's shoes (Deuteronomy 10:19).

In Christ, our core self is made new. This is the Kingdom breaking in—making things the way they should be. But much of the rest of our self, like our emotional brain, still speaks the language of this broken world (Romans 8:10). God, who originally created people to partner with him in the work of creation (Genesis 2:15), now partners with us in the re-creation of ourselves (Philippians 2:12–13). As we learn to speak the language of heaven, the broken image of God in us is restored. And the more that image of God is restored, the more the work of partnering in creation extends outside of us. Our emotional brain yearns for community, and our problem-solving brain re-wires it so that our community can come together in peace. To a world marred by conflict, we help bring *shalom*.

We become peacemakers.

We become children of God.

THINK ABOUT IT

1. In Scripture, how do we see God working for peace?

2. Do you find conflict scary? Why or why not?

3. People tend to end up in particular patterns when it comes to conflict. What conflict patterns have you experienced the most?

4. Have you ever experienced conflict that was resolved in such a way that the relationship came out stronger? How?

13

Persecuted

"Blessed are those who are persecuted because of righteousness, for theirs is the kingdom of heaven. Blessed are you when people insult you, persecute you and falsely say all kinds of evil against you because of me. Rejoice and be glad, because great is your reward in heaven, for in the same way they persecuted the prophets who were before you." (Matthew 5:10–12)

Jim Elliott knew what he was getting into. He and a coworker went to Ecuador in 1952 to evangelize some of the indigenous peoples there. They lived in the jungle, and Jim got married only because his wife Elizabeth was willing to live and share the mission with him. When he and his team (eventually five strong) decided to reach out to the Huaorani, they had no illusions about whom they were dealing with. The Huaorani were commonly called the *Auca*—the "savage." Ever since a group of rubber traders turned on them, they had been known to ambush and kill outsiders near their territory.

Despite the danger, Jim's team worked to carefully establish contact. They made weekly trips in a tiny plane dropping gifts, shouting a few welcoming phrases in the Huaorani language, and generally trying to be a friendly presence. It seemed to go well, so, on January 3, 1956, they set up a base of operations (little more than a tree house) on the Huaorani side of the river. They even received a friendly visit from three natives on January 6. Nonetheless, their radio went silent on January 8, 1956. A rescue party found all five men massacred by the very people they wanted to save.

The story may seem tragic to us, but to Jim, deliberately stepping into a situation that could, and did, claim his life was a purely rational decision. Six years earlier, he wrote in his diary, "He is no fool who gives what he cannot keep to gain that which he cannot lose."[17]

Jesus finishes the Beatitudes with, "Blessed are those who are persecuted because of righteousness, for theirs is the kingdom of heaven" (Matthew 5:10). Jesus will mention persecution again (Matthew 5:44), and that will give us a chance to look at why persecution in general happens. But looking at this beatitude (and the brief coda where Jesus discusses persecution in 5:11–12), why would "righteousness" be the thing a person gets persecuted for? Isn't righteousness a good thing?

Already in this sermon, Jesus has redefined righteousness as the living out of the Kingdom life that comes from a transformed heart. The very next section of the Sermon on the Mount after the Beatitudes (Matthew 5:13–16) is all about how living out the Kingdom life makes the followers of Jesus noticeably, visibly different. They may be different in a good way, but they are still different.

Persecution is based on being different. Without that difference, there's nothing to put a target on your back. With that difference, there is. Christians live differently from the world ("on account of righteousness"; see Matthew 5:10), and they acknowledge no higher Lord ("on account of me"; see Matthew 5:11). In a lot of places in the world, that's enough to get you killed.

This is what the prophets found out (Matthew 5:12). They stood outside the mainstream and tried to remind the people that there was a difference between the kingdom of Israel and the Kingdom of God. Jeremiah, for instance, suffered for his message (cf. Jeremiah 38:1–13), but he made it out alive. Uriah didn't (Jeremiah 26:20–23). Quite a few of the prophets came to a violent end. Jesus is clear—it's part of the package. A Nigerian woman who escaped when extremists massacred her village put it plainly: "Persecution is Scripture being fulfilled."[18]

Sesuna, a young lady in Eritrea, started a Bible study at her school and got expelled for it. When her relatives found out, she was severely beaten by her own family. According to her, "I truly learned what it was like to be an evangelical believer that day."[19]

Survey the people in your church. Ask them what it means to be a believer. Being beaten by your family is not going to be part of their answer. But Sesuna has Scripture on her side. Jesus said, "If they persecuted me, they will persecute you also" (John 15:20). By our lives, we proclaim that the kingdoms of this world are not the Kingdom of God. As Paul puts it, "We are to God the pleasing aroma of Christ among those who are being saved and those who are perishing. To the one we are an aroma that brings death; to the other, an aroma that brings life" (2 Corinthians 2:15–16). Since we are the aroma of death to those who are perishing, it's no surprise that "everyone who wants to live a godly life in Christ Jesus will be persecuted" (2 Timothy 3:12). If we never get pushback from the world, something is wrong.

This may be a factor in the current "cult of victimization" among some Christians. Persecution must be found (or fabricated) to legitimize them. Some of this persecution is imaginary. A friend of mine knew a lady who tried to post an ad on Google for vacation Bible school curriculum. When the ad got rejected, she went to Facebook to vent her frustration. Clearly, the responses asserted, Google was anti-Christian! My friend looked into it and found that Google stated exactly what words triggered the rejection—words that related to hot-button issues. He joined the comment thread to explain ways the ad could probably be revised and accepted. No good. Some of the commenters were convinced that this was an attack on Christians. My friend decided to follow that train of thought for argument's sake: "So, assuming this is actual persecution, I'm still waiting to hear the rejoicing." There was no response.

The problem with this hyperventilation about being victimized is that it disobeys the very first command in the Sermon on the Mount. In the face of persecution, Jesus says to "rejoice and be glad" (5:11).

No one is saying this is easy. During his two years in a Turkish prison, Andrew Brunson felt convicted that he was disobeying Jesus in this area. Despite his feelings, he began a discipline of rejoicing.[20] That is the attitude of someone trying to live out the Christian life.

But how could persecution possibly be a source of joy?

First, we can rejoice because persecution means we're in good company. Jesus points out the fellowship the persecuted have with the prophets. For two thousand years, Christians have looked to the fellowship they have with Jesus himself. I don't want to minimize the pain of those who have paid for their faith. I want them to see it for what it is—a chance to walk with Jesus. They can either squander the experience in anger and resentment or take the opportunity to grow closer to him. As Peter says, "Rejoice inasmuch as you participate in the sufferings of Christ, so that you may be overjoyed when his glory is revealed" (1 Peter 4:13).

The Beatitudes are framed by the persecuted and the poor in spirit. The two have a lot in common. In fact, they often experience many of the same emotions. But there's a difference. While the poor in spirit are ripe for the Kingdom because the world *failed* them, the persecuted are ripe for the Kingdom because the world is *actively rejecting* them. Jesus includes them in the Beatitudes to communicate that, despite appearances, rejection by the world is not rejection by him. It is, in fact, sharing with him.

Rejection by the world is not rejection by him.

Second, Jesus says the main reason to rejoice is because "great is your reward in heaven" (Matthew 5:11). This introduces one of the major themes of the Sermon on the Mount. There is an eternal Kingdom of Heaven which is breaking in. There is also a kingdom of this world which is doomed to pass away. Which world are you investing in?

People are persecuted for lots of things—race, nationality, class, whatever. Being persecuted for Christ has particular merit because it is usually a choice. Persecution stories are full of people who are given a chance to renounce Christ and walk away unscathed. The ones who refuse have done the cost-benefit analysis. Like Jim Elliot, they grasp the bankruptcy of this world compared to the value of the Kingdom.

The Voice of the Martyrs—an organization that ministers to persecuted Christians around the world—tells the story of an Egyptian business owner.[21] This man was solidly middle-class for his community. He gave his life to Christ. When his brothers found out, they staged a home invasion. They restrained him in his own house and gave him three choices: he could renounce Christ, they could kill him on the spot, or he could sign all his business and personal property over to them and leave with nothing. He faced the choice, as clearly as one possibly could.

And this respected businessman walked out his front door in his underwear.

He

left

everything.

It's not just the world actively rejecting the persecuted. The persecuted are actively rejecting *the world*.

> There were others who were tortured, refusing to be released. . . Some faced jeers and flogging, and even chains and imprisonment. They were put to death by stoning, they were sawed in two; they were killed by the sword. They went about in sheepskins and goatskins, destitute, persecuted and mistreated. . . . They wandered in deserts and mountains, living in caves and in holes in the ground. . . . They were foreigners and strangers on earth. . . . If they had been thinking of the country they had left, they would have had opportunity to return. Instead, they were longing for a better country—a heavenly one. (Hebrews 11:35–38, 13–16)

Unlike comfortable Americans, the persecuted no longer get to pretend that they can have the Kingdom *and* the world. They are no longer trying to organize their lives around comfort and risk-avoidance. The choice is put to them starkly—the world, or the Kingdom?

And they choose the Kingdom.

THINK ABOUT IT

1. In what ways do we sometimes try to have both the Kingdom and the world?

2. What are the reasons Jesus gave for why we should rejoice when persecuted?

3. Try to imagine "rejoicing" because of persecution. What would your mindset have to be for this to make sense?

4. What might "rejecting the world" look like in your life?

14

Salt and Light

*"You are the salt of the earth. But if the salt loses its saltiness,
how can it be made salty again? It is no longer good for
anything, except to be thrown out and trampled underfoot.
"You are the light of the world. A town built on a hill cannot
be hidden. Neither do people light a lamp and put it under
a bowl. Instead they put it on its stand, and it gives light
to everyone in the house. In the same way, let your light
shine before others, that they may see your good deeds
and glorify your Father in heaven."* (Matthew 5:13–16)

After I left professional ministry, going into retail was not a soft landing. My second day as Assistant Department Manager of Cabinets and Appliances, a guy threatened to punch me because his special-order countertop hadn't arrived yet. Working at the intersection of people, their possessions, and their money, we don't always see people at their best. No manager actually says, "The customer is always right," but childish behavior can get a person pretty far.

It's a tough environment. New team members would finish our Manager Trainee program bright-eyed and ready to go. I gave them two weeks before the place broke them. The way to survive was to become bitter and hard. Like I did. Customers would bark at me, and I would bark right back. Then I would immediately go and talk to my coworkers about them. I'm not going to repeat the kinds of things we said about customers behind their backs. Self-disclosure has its limits.

Commiserating with coworkers was fun enough, but I eventually noticed that, in conversations with my friends at work, I avoided mentioning my faith. I had to admit that the reason I didn't talk about my faith was because my behavior was an embarrassment. If my life was a demonstration of what Jesus does for a person, why would anyone want that? They could find that kind of behavior anywhere.

Convicted, I let Jesus speak to me about my attitude. I started researching and practicing ways to reflect him better. It was tough work, but I knew I was making progress when one of my gay friends spontaneously said that he saw me as someone whose life was consistent with his beliefs. Getting this reaction was both gratifying and humbling.

But evangelism still didn't happen. A popular model nowadays says that we should make friends, they will see that we are different, and eventually they will ask us why. That's not what I experienced. Oh, I eventually had plenty of spiritual conversations with my coworkers, but they were never about the merits of Christianity. Most of our conversations about Christians basically asked, "What is wrong with those people?" I wasn't evangelizing. I was apologizing.

In my effort to witness to my friends, I began to realize that there was a much larger problem. In my setting—largely white, middle-class America—my friends did not see Christians as salt and light.

In Matthew 5:13–16, Jesus says:

> You are the salt of the earth. But if the salt loses its saltiness, how can it be made salty again? It is no longer good for anything, except to be thrown out and trampled underfoot. You are the light of the world. A town built on a hill cannot be hidden. Neither do people light a lamp and put it under a bowl. Instead they put it on its stand, and it gives light to everyone in the house. In the same way, let your light shine before others, that they may see your good deeds and glorify your Father in heaven.

Much handwringing has gone into figuring out what characteristic of salt Jesus is talking about. Salt can be a seasoning, but it can also be a preservative. The idea that believers have a preserving effect on the world around them is a nice theological note. It has scriptural support (Genesis 18:20–32; Acts 27:21–25). But it doesn't really fit the parallelism Jesus sets up between "salt" and "light." The obvious feature of light is that you notice it. It makes a distinct difference. Salt as flavoring has that immediate impact in a way that salt as preservative doesn't. If you add salt to something you're eating, you notice the difference immediately. Just like if you turn the lights on in a room. (Also, the verb Jesus uses in 5:13 could be translated "become bland.")

So Jesus is saying that people who live out the Kingdom life are distinctly different. The difference is noticeable—in a good way. Dropping the metaphor, the result is "that [the world] may see your good deeds and glorify your Father in heaven" (Matthew 5:16). If we are transformed by Christ, our "deeds" make God look better, not worse.

People who live out the Kingdom life are distinctly different.

But what good deeds? Like most things in the Sermon on the Mount, Jesus takes our understanding of "good deeds" and turns it completely inside out. The Sermon on the Mount has two major discussions about things we should do—one on fulfilling the heart of the law (Matthew 5:21–48) and one on avoiding a religious show (Matthew 6:1–18). When Jesus introduces the discussion in chapter 6, he calls visible religious acts—giving, praying, and fasting—"righteousness" (Matthew 6:1). Elsewhere he refers to almost the exact same things as "deeds" (Matthew 23:5). So it's tempting to conclude that giving, praying, and fasting are the "good deeds" that bring glory to God when the world sees them.

Except they're not.

The "good deeds" of 5:16 can't be the "righteousness" of 6:1 because the whole point of Jesus' teaching in chapter 6 is to keep those things to yourself. Do them in secret so that the world doesn't see them (Matthew 6:1). (The world just thinks they're weird, anyway. It's not impressed.)

The natural place to look for "good deeds" would be the discussion that immediately follows 5:16 in the rest of chapter 5. It's easy to overlook this section since its focus is not on outward actions but on the heart—on inward character.

True, you can't see character directly. But what's inside works its way out (Matthew 7:16–18). The heart attitudes Jesus describes reveal themselves to the world in the way we treat others. This is what Jesus wants the world to see—hearts transformed by him (cf. 1 Peter 2:12).

Respecting others by refusing to have contempt for our brothers (Matthew 5:21–26) and refusing to objectify our sisters (Matthew 5:27–32); communicating sincerely (Matthew 5:33–37); living from a heart of grace (Matthew 5:38–42); loving universally (Matthew 5:43–48)—this way of living is distinctly different. The world notices it. And it makes things better.

When the world sees us living this way, it begins to think that God might not be so bad after all.

So is that what the world is seeing?

I realize we're fighting uphill on this one. The "rigid, angry religious person" is a convenient literary trope. This stereotype generates a lot of internet clicks. However, if it ran counter to most people's experience, it would ring hollow. But it doesn't. So we need to ask ourselves two questions.

First, *is the world even seeing us?* Or have we become invisible by walling ourselves into our colonial-era missionary compounds? We have our own social get-togethers and meeting places, our own schools, our own entertainment, our own news, even our own business directories. We have everything we need to do life without interacting with those filthy pagans. If this sounds familiar . . . *stop it*. It is direct disobedience against Jesus' command, "*Let your light shine*" (Matthew 5:16).

Learn your neighbor's names. Talk to the people you encounter at work. Even better, listen to them. If you enjoy a hobby, join a club. Revive the ancient practice of having people over for dinner. If you're really ambitious, the gold standard for building cross-cultural understanding is to work together toward shared goals. However you do it, hang out with people who are not of your tribe.

The second question is a lot harder: *Are we being transformed?* A city on a hill is easy to miss if there aren't any lights on. I was interviewing for a position at a Bible college once, and one of the faculty members commented, "I keep hearing people talk about transformation, but I'm not sure what that actually means." I responded, "I think it means growing in our ability to love God and other people." I wanted to add, "If that isn't happening, everything we're doing here is a waste of time."

A friend of mine once asked a retired minister, "In all your decades of ministry, how many lives did you see truly changed?" His answer: "Two."

In his interview for *The Unfolding* podcast,[22] Brant Hanson talked about meeting for coffee with his former youth minister and mentor. The man had since left the faith because the Christian story says that people should change, but he didn't see people changing. This triggered a faith crisis for Brant himself. It's a question we need to seriously ask ourselves: Are we seeing Christians radically transformed so that they live out the Kingdom life? Or is Christianity just a convenient framework for constructing our tribal identity?

Brant didn't resolve his question until he did some work overseas. There he found Christians who were following what Jesus taught—things like praying for their enemies. As Brant puts it, they were actually "doing the stuff." They were distinctly, noticeably different, and Christ was present so powerfully that miracles were happening. The story works.

The problem with the relative lack of transformation my friends see in the Christians around them is not with the universal church itself. It may be a problem with the *American* church. The world does not see our light because, on the whole, the American church may be deeply sick. That's no good because Jesus' discussion includes a very serious warning: "But if the salt loses its saltiness, how can it be made salty again? It is no longer good for anything, except to be thrown out and trampled underfoot" (Matthew 5:13).

Forget all the chemistry involved—that salt can't actually lose its saltiness. But if it were possible, if it could lose the property of taste but not any of the others, how would you fix it? Add salt? It's done. You're not going to put that in your food anymore. All you can do with it now is use it to kill the weeds on your walking path. To put it in contemporary terms, there are places (including America) where Christianity has become a toxic brand. Good luck selling that.

The only hope we have of turning this thing around is to live out Jesus' words. As Brant says, we need to start "doing the stuff." Let the Kingdom take hold of us, shake us, convict us, change us. Otherwise, we're just offering more of the same. But the world doesn't need more darkness. It doesn't need more banality.

It needs us to be transformed.

1. Have you seen Christians portrayed negatively in our culture? Have you seen any behavior from Christians that makes this portrayal believable?

2. Why do you think God makes his reputation dependent on his people?

3. Have you ever felt that you represented Christ poorly? What have you done to try and change that?

4. Has anyone ever indicated that you represented Christ well? What effect did it have?

15

Fulfilling the Law

"Do not think that I have come to abolish the Law or the Prophets; I have not come to abolish them but to fulfill them. For truly I tell you, until heaven and earth disappear, not the smallest letter, not the least stroke of a pen will by any means disappear from the Law until everything is accomplished. Therefore anyone who sets aside one of the least of these commands and teaches others accordingly will be called least in the kingdom of heaven, but whoever practices and teaches these commands will be called great in the kingdom of heaven. For I tell you that unless your righteousness surpasses that of the Pharisees and the teachers of the law, you will certainly not enter the kingdom of heaven." (Matthew 5:17–20)

When I try to puzzle out the relationship between the old and new covenants, I am always in imaginary dialogue with my good friend Dave. Years ago, Dave went on a tour of Israel led by a guy who was (effectively) a Messianic Jewish rabbi. Afterward, Dave was convicted that, as a Christ-follower, he should keep the Sabbath. He did, and things snowballed from there. Now Dave and his family do everything they can to literally follow the Torah. The depth this has added to his spiritual life is obvious and impressive.

Dave understands grace, and he doesn't expect all Christians to live the way he does. Well . . . at least he doesn't out loud or in public. Deep down, he is convinced that there is no good excuse for Christians to not live according to Torah.

Traditionally, Christian thought has swung in the opposite direction. In the second century, some of the early church fathers thought the Old Testament was weird, kind of pointless, and should be cut out of the Bible entirely. (Some of them were, like many Romans, horribly anti-Semitic.) This anti-Semitism was strong throughout the Reformation, so Torah observance was often explicitly discouraged.

Which position is right—Christian tradition in its more hard-nosed moments or Dave in his? Jesus doesn't fit either one comfortably. The Pharisees obviously weren't happy with his handling of the Law. He wasn't simply rubber-stamping it. On the other hand, in Matthew 5:17–20, Jesus says, as clearly as possible, that he is not abolishing it.

He says that he came to fulfill it.

> Do not think that I have come to abolish the Law or the Prophets; I have not come to abolish them but to fulfill them. For truly I tell you, until heaven and earth disappear, not the smallest letter, not the least stroke of a pen will by any means disappear from the Law until everything is accomplished. Therefore anyone who sets aside one of the least of these commands and teaches others accordingly will be called least in the kingdom of heaven, but whoever practices and teaches these commands will be called great in the kingdom of heaven. For I tell you that unless your righteousness surpasses that of the Pharisees and the teachers of the law, you will certainly not enter the kingdom of heaven. (Matthew 5:17–20)

Jesus is talking to a Jewish audience here. The Law was the organizing center for their entire lives, delivered to Moses on the top of Mount Sinai. You don't mess with the Law. But Jesus sure seems to be messin'. He's about to quote the Law and then say, "*But* I tell you . . ." (Matthew 5:21–48). Before he gets started, he wants to be as clear as possible in Matthew 5:17–20—he is *not* giving the Law the boot.

We can think of the Law two ways (ways that Israelites themselves would not have separated out): first as legally binding rules, and second as ethical teaching. The book of Deuteronomy leans heavily on the legal sense. The book takes the standard contemporary form for a covenant between an emperor and a new vassal state: it rehearses the history between the two, gives a bunch of rules for how the emperor wants his new subjects to behave, then lists good things he will do if they follow the rules and bad things he will do if they don't. So, in slightly anachronistic terms, we can think of the Law almost like a constitution—the controlling document for how this relationship works.

This points us toward some of the ways Jesus fulfills the Law, but it's complicated. The distinction between the two ages—the old age that is doomed to pass away and the new age that is breaking in—is the driving force of Paul's letter to the Galatians. He introduces his letter by praising God for rescuing us "from the *present evil age*" (Galatians 1:4). His final summary of the letter is that "what counts is the *new creation*" (Galatians 6:15). Old age/new age.

Throughout the letter, Paul juxtaposes characteristics of the "present evil age" that we've been rescued from against characteristics of the "new creation" that we are now a part of. On the "old" side of this line, we find things like the flesh, slavery, and destruction. On the "new" side, we find the Spirit, freedom, and life (Galatians 5:16–17; 4:31–5:1; 6:8). Which side is the Law on? Every time it is mentioned, the Law is solidly placed on the side of "this present evil age."

This doesn't mean that the Law is bad. It means that it functions as the controlling document for the people of God *in the world that is passing away.*

As someone born under the Law, Jesus took the curse of the Law (Galatians 3:13). Christian thinking has gotten confused about what "the curse of the law" is, but Paul is not subtle about what he means. There are two whole chapters in Deuteronomy (Deuteronomy 27–28) that are all about "blessings and curses." The point in these chapters is simple. In fact, it's explicitly stated at the end of Deuteronomy 27, and Paul quotes it as a way of referencing those two chapters: "Cursed is everyone who does not continue to do everything written in the Book of the Law" (Galatians 3:10; Deuteronomy 27:26). What are these curses? All the nasty stuff in Deuteronomy 28—the things that start with "*cursed* will you be . . ."! If you don't keep the Law, bad stuff will happen. That's the agreement.

But here's what Paul noticed: The Law itself says that you are cursed if you are hung on a tree (Deuteronomy 21:23). Jesus was hung on a tree. But you are cursed if you break the Law. Jesus didn't break the Law. In fact, he was sinless (John 8:46). An Israelite could sin, go through the appropriate steps to make atonement, and still come out with the status of "blameless." "Sinless" is a standard that even the Law wasn't looking for. But Jesus met it. He may have put some of the Pharisees' traditions in the blender, but he followed the Law itself to the letter.

So (reasons Paul) on the cross, Jesus was being cursed. Since he didn't break the Law, he must be taking the curse for someone else (Galatians 3:13). As Messiah, the one who embodies Israel, he's taking the curse for everyone else. He is "the Lamb of God, who takes away the sin of the world" (John 1:29).

On the cross, Jesus took the full curse of the Law. So where does that leave the Law? The deal was, if you break the Law, you get cursed. Israel broke the Law, and Jesus took the curse. So . . . what's left? It seems like it's done. It's run its course. "For through the law, I died to the law" (Galatians 2:19). What the Law said *has* "come to pass" (Matthew 5:18).

On the cross, Jesus took the full curse of the Law.

Also, to some extent, heaven and earth *have* passed away (Matthew 5:18). In the cross, something cosmic took place. When Jesus died, the entire old age died with him. When he rose, he rose as the first representative of the new age (Colossians 1:18; Revelation 1:5). This new age becomes a reality for anyone who is "in him" (2 Corinthians 5:17). It may seem like a stretch to say that this is what Jesus means by "until heaven and earth disappear" (Matthew 5:18), but Peter quotes similar language on Pentecost: "I will show wonders in the heavens above. . . . The sun will be turned to darkness and the moon to blood" (Acts 2:19–20; Joel 2:30–31). Peter says that this is what his audience is seeing (Acts 2:16). The outpouring of the Spirit on Pentecost is a visible sign of the passing of one age and the beginning of another. Apocalyptic language is entirely appropriate.

The prophets saw that this new age would bring a new covenant—a new agreement between God and his people (Jeremiah 31:31–34). The word Hebrews uses when discussing Jeremiah 31 (Hebrews 8:13) means "new, of a different kind." It's not replacing an apple with another apple. It's replacing the apple with an orange. Paul, in Galatians, contrasts the two covenants (Galatians 4:24) and the two ages. For those living in the new covenant, he talks about fulfilling the "Law of Christ" (Galatians 6:2). In the new covenant, it's not that Jesus nullifies the Law; he is the Law. In the new covenant, the controlling document for the people of God is Jesus himself.

But seriously, the Old Testament Law takes up a good chunk of our Bibles. What are we supposed to do with it? Well, if you want to know God's heart, study it. As instruction (the second way to look at the Law), the Law was always intended to be a revelation of God's heart.

Leviticus, one of the most regulation-heavy books in the Old Testament, is peppered with the phrase, "Be holy as I am holy" (e.g., Leviticus 19:2). The point is that these rules God gave Israel weren't arbitrary. God wasn't like, "Hmm . . . should murder be right or wrong? I'll go with wrong." The rules are based on principles, and those principles are, in turn, based on the very character of God. For instance, murder is wrong because God is life. The rules reveal God's heart. As people follow them, they learn to be holy as he is holy.

This is one reason it's never a good idea to discourage anyone from following them (Matthew 5:19). It's also why Paul himself is still celebrating the Jewish feasts (Acts 20:16) and even sponsoring sacrifices decades after the crucifixion (Acts 21:24). Because the Law points to God and is fulfilled in Christ, early Christianity had no trouble incorporating Jews who were still "zealous for the law" (Acts 21:20–21). The Law can point people to God's heart.

It can, but that doesn't mean it necessarily will. A person could follow all the rules but make no connection with the deeper principles, much less God's heart. The prophets spent a lot of time pointing this out. Ancient Israel often focused on getting the sacrifices right, while overlooking being the kind of people God called them to be (Micah 6:6–8). Sometimes they just flat-out ignored some of the laws. Well, the Pharisees fixed that. But nit-picking about the letter of the law still didn't get them to the heart of God. This was the core of Jesus' problem with them (cf. Matthew 23:16–28).

This is what Jesus means by, "Unless your righteousness surpasses that of the Pharisees and the teachers of the law, you will certainly not enter the kingdom of heaven" (Matthew 5:20). The failure of the ultimate rule-keepers to take on the heart of God shows the failure of focusing on rule-keeping itself.

That's the tragedy of thinking that the rest of Matthew 5 is just Jesus giving an even stricter set of rules. In Matthew 5:21–48, Jesus calls out the fancy footwork people do to keep the letter of the law while missing the heart. Make his statements into a new list of rules, and people will find a way to dance around them too. Instead, Jesus is pointing to the heart.

This calls for a new covenant—one that can put the principles of the Law, the spirit of the Law, on people's hearts (Jer. 31:33; cf. 2 Corinthians 3:6). Paul compares the Law to a guardian (*paidagogos*), training and supervising the kids until they grow up (Galatians 3:23–25). This mirrors people's actual moral development. Kids need rules. They have no clue what's a good idea, what's a bad idea, or how they should be in the world. They need something external to guide them. But growing up involves internalizing the principles involved in these rules. Once people have a strong moral compass, they don't need to refer to rules all that much.

It seems like God did this with humanity. Israel was grateful for the Law because they saw that it gave them a leg-up on the nations around them (Psalms 19:7–12; 119:1–16). The Creator of the universe had given them guidance on how to be in the world. So, as Paul says, "The law is holy, and the commandment is holy, righteous and good" (Romans 7:12). The only problem, which Paul hammers at brutally, is that the written Law was external. It couldn't change anyone. (But it surely could condemn them!)

Looked at in the best light, the Law raised people up and trained them until, in the new covenant, they grew up. People could get a new heart, and then they could live the heart of God from the inside out.

This doesn't nullify the Law, however. The spirit of the Law is what matters. Jesus and Paul both seem to argue that to fulfill the spirit of the Law is to fulfill the Law. What else could be the point of statements like, "Whoever loves others has fulfilled the law" (Romans 13:10)? Or, "Do to others what you would have them do to you, for this sums up the Law and the Prophets" (Matthew 7:12)?

If we live out the heart of God, we're fulfilling the Law. This, after all, is what the Law was aiming at all along.

THINK ABOUT IT

1. Have you spent much time looking at the Old Testament Law, or do you generally avoid it? Why?

2. How was giving the Law an act of love on God's part?

3. Why do people gravitate toward rules-based religion?

4. If Jesus took the curse of the Law, why should we try to be holy?

16

Contempt

"You have heard that it was said to the people long ago, 'You shall not murder, and anyone who murders will be subject to judgment.' But I tell you that anyone who is angry with a brother or sister will be subject to judgment. Again, anyone who says to a brother or sister, 'Raca,' is answerable to the court. And anyone who says, 'You fool!' will be in danger of the fire of hell. Therefore, if you are offering your gift at the altar and there remember that your brother or sister has something against you, leave your gift there in front of the altar. First go and be reconciled to them; then come and offer your gift. Settle matters quickly with your adversary who is taking you to court. Do it while you are still together on the way, or your adversary may hand you over to the officer, and you may be thrown into prison. Truly I tell you, you will not get out until you have paid the last penny." (Matthew 5:21–26)

I heard a lot of conservative talk radio growing up. Name-calling was ubiquitous. "Liberal" itself became a pejorative term, but specific situations sometimes called for more creative epithets like "feminazi." More often, they were just "idiots."

In Matthew 5:21–23, Jesus connects name-calling and anger. In those afternoon radio shows, anger was clearly present. One time, a caller asked a question pointing away from the show's received wisdom, and the host just shouted him down. It was a real turning point for me. I realized, "Wait a second. He didn't actually answer that guy's question. He just barked a bunch of catch phrases at him." The host's response to the caller was the verbal equivalent of roaring at him until he went away.

This general attitude fertilized the ground for its audience until, on January 6, 2021, hundreds of them attacked the United States Capitol. They assaulted at least 140 police officers while calling for the deaths of public officials. Some of them came with murder on their lips. And people died.[23]

Jesus is right—there is an attitude that draws a line from name-calling to anger to murder.

Going straight for one of the Ten Commandments, Jesus starts the meat of the Sermon on the Mount with a bedrock moral principle—one that most cultures would agree on—murder is bad. We're all on the same page there.

That's good, because that page is about to get flipped.

> You have heard that it was said to the people long ago, "You shall not murder, and anyone who murders will be subject to judgment." But I tell you that anyone who is angry with a brother or sister will be subject to judgment. Again, anyone who says to a brother or sister, "Raca," is answerable to the court. And anyone who says, "You fool!" will be in danger of the fire of hell. (Matthew 5:21–23)

To understand how Jesus connects murder to anger and name-calling (Matthew 5:21–22), we have to remember that Jesus is not interested in just tightening up the rules. This is fairly easy to see when it comes to name-calling. He says not to call a brother "Raca" or "fool." In nice Hebrew parallelism, these are basically synonymous. One is Aramaic, the other is Greek, but they are both harsh ways of saying that someone is "empty-headed" or "stupid."

We know that Jesus is going deeper than simply saying that we should avoid these particular words. In fact, most of the uses of "fool" in the New Testament come from Jesus himself (cf. Matthew 7:26; 23:17; 25:2). There's an attitude involved here.

The same is true for anger. It's unrealistic and unhealthy to simply say, "Anger is bad." So we twist ourselves into pretzels trying to delineate what kind of anger is okay and what kind isn't. That's not the point. Paul makes a distinction between anger and sin, "In your anger, do not sin" (Ephesians 4:26), implying that you can be angry without sinning. In this verse, Paul uses the same word Jesus uses in Matthew 5:22. Therefore, anger is not inherently bad. Again, we're looking at an underlying attitude.

What attitude do murder and name-calling have in common? If murder is on one end of the spectrum and name-calling is on the other, what is the spectrum? Contempt. Hold on to anger for too long (Ephesians 4:26), and you get contempt.

Expressing contempt is the basic linguistic function of calling someone a pejorative name. Name-calling is a way to "other" someone, to make them "less than." It devalues another human being. It says that someone who is created in the image of God, who is infinitely and inherently valuable, is just one of those "idiots."

Murder is the ultimate act of contempt. It reduces the value of that life to zero. Murder and name-calling may be on opposite ends of the "contempt" spectrum, but Jesus is pointing out that they are on the same spectrum nonetheless. In our hearts, what's the difference between making someone dead and thinking that they may as well be? To be appalled at one while enjoying the other is to keep the letter of the law while totally missing its heart.

Again, in the same parallel statements, Jesus points out that this mindset is going to get us into trouble with both God and people (Matthew 5:22).

> Anyone who says to a brother or sister, "Raca," is answerable to the court. And anyone who says, "You fool!" will be in danger of the fire of hell. Therefore, if you are offering your gift at the altar and there remember that your brother or sister has something against you, leave your gift there in front of the altar. First go and be reconciled to them; then come and offer your gift. Settle matters quickly with your adversary who is taking you to court. Do it while you are still together on the way, or your adversary may hand you over to the officer, and you may be thrown into prison. Truly I tell you, you will not get out until you have paid the last penny. (Matthew 5:21–26)

Matthew 5:22 starts off a chiasm—a literary form that Jesus seems quite fond of. The basic structure of this chiasm is A B B A. It looks like this:

A: people (the Sanhedrin)

B: God (the fires of Gehenna) (5:22)

B: God (offering a sacrifice) (5:23–24)

A: people (going to court) (5:25–26)

First, Jesus discusses getting into trouble with God. As we saw in chapter 11, the whole purpose of the sacrificial system is fellowship with God. Worshipers deal with their sin so they can draw near to him. The capstone is the fellowship offering, part of which becomes a feast that the worshippers symbolically share with God himself. So, in Matthew 5:23, we have someone presuming to draw near to God while harboring contempt for a brother. That's not how fellowship with God works. John constantly returns to the theme, "Whoever claims to love God yet hates a brother or sister is a liar" (1 John 4:20). If we don't love our brother, we're not sharing God's heart.

For the church in Corinth, Paul makes the reasoning even more explicit. If our brothers and sisters are the body of Christ, thinking that we can commune with him while despising them isn't even logically coherent. People were presuming to draw near to God, enjoying the Lord's Supper, a feast that called back to the very sacrifice that reconciled them to God, while showing contempt for each other (1 Corinthians 11:18–22). Paul tells them, "Everyone ought to examine themselves before they eat of the bread and drink from the cup" (1 Corinthians 11:28). This self-examination consists of "discerning the body of the Lord" (11:29). What is that "body"? The person sitting next to them. The one they have contempt for. Paul agrees with Jesus—they need to get their heart right concerning the other person first. Otherwise, whatever they're doing doesn't even count as the "Lord's Supper" (11:20).

> **If we don't love our brother, we're not sharing God's heart.**

Drawing near to God should prompt us to examine our hearts. If there is contempt for our brother or sister, we need to invite God to deal with that. If our heart isn't right with our brother or sister, it's not right with him. So if we have contempt for someone when we draw near to God but are not convicted about it, we are blinding ourselves. God is trying to get our attention, and we are refusing to yield. In choosing to hold on to contempt, we're just putting on a performance when we draw near to God. But thinking that we and God are cool when we are not is dangerous. The Corinthians were doing that, and they were paying for it (1 Corinthians 11:30).

Second, contempt can also get us into trouble with *people* because it can blind us to our own guilt (Matthew 5:25–26). There is a self-justifying cycle here. Our anger justifies our contempt, and our contempt justifies our anger. Our contempt also justifies treating others as "less than." As our actions degrade them, this justifies and intensifies our contempt. If we keep this cycle of contempt going long enough, we dehumanize them. We stop seeing them as people. Contempt eventually justifies treating someone in a way we would never treat a fully human, inherently valuable person.[24]

It's common for criminals to justify the harm they have done by finding reasons to view their victims with contempt. Blind to the horror of their actions, they say their victim simply "had it coming."

That works fine until you're standing in front of a judge.

Take the guy in Matthew 5:25: "Settle matters quickly with your adversary who is taking you to court. Do it while you are still together on the way, or your adversary may hand you over to the judge, and the judge may hand you over to the officer, and you may be thrown into prison." Surely this person knows he owes the other guy money. Why doesn't he just settle accounts? Unless Jesus has changed subject mid-chiasm, maybe it's because this guy views his "adversary" with contempt. In his mind, this adversary doesn't deserve to be paid back. Looking through his lens of contempt, he doesn't see that he's done anything wrong.

Judges who aren't looking through this lens of contempt see things very differently. We should do some serious soul-searching before we end up in court because at that point, it's too late. Just ask the January 6 Capitol rioters. After marinating in contempt for months and years, they seriously thought there was nothing wrong with their actions, up to and including those who went in intending to physically harm others. Many of them laughed all the way to court. And they paid for it.

Contempt isn't new, but it is an epidemic of our time. It makes for great ratings. How many reality shows thrive precisely because we love to feel superior to the people in them? How much news is a thinly-veiled version of George Orwell's "Two Minute Hate"—the two minutes a day when everyone lines their chairs up in front of the telescreen to rage at caricatured images of their supposed adversaries?[25] But for us, it's not two minutes. It's 24/7. Our culture is suffocating in the smog of contempt.

Contempt is not entertainment. It is not information. It is death. It is the exact opposite of the Kingdom. We desperately need to come up for air.

How? Remember: Jesus thought the person you despise was worth dying for. The call of the Kingdom is not to learn to have contempt for the right people. It is to end contempt by grasping that every human being has the value of one created in the image of God.

THINK ABOUT IT

1. Where do you see contempt encouraged in our culture?

2. Have you ever held on to anger for a long time? What happened?

3. Has anyone treated you with contempt? Did they call you a specific "name"? How did that feel?

4. Is there any person you need to apologize to or any group you have viewed with contempt for which you need to repent?

17

Objectification

"You have heard that it was said, 'You shall not commit adultery.'
But I tell you that anyone who looks at a woman lustfully has
already committed adultery with her in his heart. If your right
eye causes you to stumble, gouge it out and throw it away. It is
better for you to lose one part of your body than for your whole
body to be thrown into hell. And if your right hand causes you
to stumble, cut it off and throw it away. It is better for you to lose
one part of your body than for your whole body to go into hell.
It has been said, 'Anyone who divorces his wife must give
her a certificate of divorce.' But I tell you that anyone who
divorces his wife, except for sexual immorality, makes
her the victim of adultery, and anyone who marries a
divorced woman commits adultery." (Matthew 5:27–32)

People have sex drives. This may come as a surprise to folks who, like me, grew up sheltered in the church. When I was a teenager, the message seemed to be, "If you realize you have a sex drive, for heaven's sake, turn that thing off until you get married!" That approach is comically inadequate for an impulse that is just a hair less basic, universal, and compelling than eating.

Let me tell a story to demonstrate my naivete. Not too long ago, the subject came up in a church small group, and I mentioned a cashier I knew at work. The cashiers were typically attractive, college-aged women. I have no idea how we didn't get sued for that, but it made the day go by easier. After a few conversations, I started forming a high opinion of one particular young lady. She was a self-motivated, strong, conscientious worker. She seemed to have her head on straight and know where she was going in life. So it was a dose of reality when she talked about waking up to an alarm that morning and realizing that it was her boyfriend's. My heart sank. My immediate reaction was, "If this young lady, who seems so sensible and put-together, takes for granted that moving in with your boyfriend is just what you do, then it's *everyone*."

After sharing this story with my church small group, you could hear the crickets. "Oh," I realized. "It's all of you, too."

When it comes to sexuality, it's hard to imagine an area in which the church is doing a worse job of presenting a compelling vision to our culture. That's a shame because the Bible has a lot of practical, ground-level wisdom on the subject.

In our culture, sexual morality hinges entirely on *consent*. If you don't have consent, sex is bad. If you do have consent, anything goes. Biblically, sexual morality hinges on whether the relationship mirrors God's relationship with his people (Ephesians 5:25–32). As we've been saying, biblical morality, in general, is about mirroring the heart of God. In Scripture, the characteristic of God most emphasized regarding sexual relationships is *faithfulness* (e.g., Malachi 2:13–16).

Human beings are physical, emotional, intellectual, volitional (able to make deliberate choices), and spiritual. We can grow closer to someone on any of those levels. A biblical sexual ethic hinges on volitional closeness—*faithfulness*—an unconditional commitment to each other. When this commitment is present, the spiritual union that takes place in sex (1 Corinthians 6:16) can integrate our physical, emotional, and intellectual selves to invite *shalom*. We could call this "holistic sex." Without this commitment, these aspects are integrated dysfunctionally, setting them up to be torn apart violently and painfully. (The word "unite" in 1 Corinthians 6:16 is derived from the word for glue.) Sex can either be the place where all aspects of our humanity are most integrated or the place where they are most torn apart.

Rather than approaching sexuality from this "big picture" perspective, Jesus is looking at a particular angle in Matthew 5:27–32:

> You have heard that it was said, "You shall not commit adultery." But I tell you that anyone who looks at a woman lustfully has already

committed adultery with her in his heart. If your right eye causes you to stumble, gouge it out and throw it away. It is better for you to lose one part of your body than for your whole body to be thrown into hell. And if your right hand causes you to stumble, cut it off and throw it away. It is better for you to lose one part of your body than for your whole body to go into hell.

It has been said, "Anyone who divorces his wife must give her a certificate of divorce." But I tell you that anyone who divorces his wife, except for sexual immorality, makes her the victim of adultery, and anyone who marries a divorced woman commits adultery.

As in the previous paragraph in Matthew 5, Jesus draws another spectrum to show how people can try to keep the letter of the law but miss its heart. On one end of the spectrum, we have adultery. Adultery is bad. Even our culture agrees on that. "Cheaters" are not regarded highly. The other end of the spectrum is "looking." Our culture is very ambiguous about "looking."

Jesus is talking about looking *with intent*. A literal translation of Matthew 5:28 says that someone "looks at a woman *for the purpose of* desiring her." (Compare the parallel construction in 6:1, where people perform their acts of righteousness *for the purpose of* being seen by others.) Note: women can do this, too, but we'll stick with the pronouns because this tends to be a characteristically male problem.

This looking isn't just noticing a pretty lady. You can look at something beautiful—say a sunset—without wanting to possess it, own it, consume it. That's because we are wired to admire something like that, but that's all. Not so with women. We also have fundamental wiring concerned with mating. In fact, you can often feel that switch flipping; you experience a rush of relevant hormones and go into "consume" mode.

The part of our brains concerned with mating is primal and way faster than the part that makes conscious decisions. This means that this initial "looking" (and any resulting hormone dump) happens with no intent whatsoever. Which means it's not what Jesus is talking about. There's nothing wrong with it. As I said to my boys when it was time to start talking about such things, "It's okay for women to be pretty, and it's okay for women to be interesting. That's how God made us."

What matters is what happens next.

It doesn't take all that long for us to become consciously aware of what's happening. At that point, we can either dial it down or look away. If we look again knowing full well the reaction we're going to have, we shouldn't kid ourselves. We are looking *with intent*. We're looking because we want to go into "consume mode."

That's not okay, because we consume *things*, not people. This way of looking is, by definition, objectification. First, it sees women primarily (if not entirely) in terms of the physical. Yes, our bodies are part of us, and they do say something about who we are. But the most important stuff is stuff we don't see—a person's thoughts and emotions, their history and attitudes, their hopes, fears, and dreams. To ignore all of that is to treat them as less than fully human.

Second, it instrumentalizes them. Rather than dignifying people as an end in themselves, it treats them as a means. It sees them mostly in terms of what they can do for us. Who cares what the repercussions for them are?

This is what puts "looking with intent" on the same continuum as adultery. This spectrum is the spectrum of *objectification*. To commit the sin of unfaithfulness is to break a commitment. The adulterer can justify this only by reducing both wife and mistress to what they can do for him. If his wife isn't satisfying him, maybe a mistress will. He doesn't see these women as ends in themselves. They are means. They are objects.

If he's just concerned about the letter of the law, he can weasel out of this by divorcing one woman to marry the other. The short paragraph on divorce (Matthew 5:31–32) is not a new discussion. It is tied to the first paragraph (5:27–30) by continuing the language of "adultery," and the introductory connectives—"It has been said"—are far weaker than any of the other paragraphs here at the end of chapter 5. This scenario of divorce is an illustration of the larger principle.

It is particularly objectifying to swap a wife out for a newer model. It is instrumentalizing because, in the culture of Jesus' day, a man usually looked for a divorce because his wife wasn't giving him children. Her value didn't come from who she was, but from what she could produce.

What happens to the divorced woman in Matthew 5:32 is a little hard to translate. It's a passive form of the verb "to commit adultery." Perhaps we could translate it, "He makes her to be *adulterated*." If she committed sexual immorality, she adulterated herself. Fair enough. But here, through no fault of her own, she has to carry that stigma into the world. In Jesus' culture, particularly, she would be viewed as damaged goods. The husband doesn't care, because he's preoccupied with what these women can or can't do for him.

This is objectifying, and it is not the heart of God.

"Too right!" yells our culture, "How dare he treat her like that!" But this is where our culture tries to have its cake and eat it, too. The "Me Too" movement tried very hard, first, to raise awareness of the pervasive plague of objectification and, second, to create a cultural consensus that objectification is not okay. But why does our culture think objectification is not okay? For the same reason it considers any sexual act not okay: lack of consent. The women being harassed, assaulted, or otherwise objectified are not giving consent. So our culture's position is not that objectification itself is bad, but that *non-consensual* objectification is bad.

Consensual sex workers know that they are being objectified. They signed on for that (at least in the best-case scenario). So, by splitting things down the line of consent, our culture wants to safeguard the consent and dignity of women (as in the "Me Too" movement) and casually commoditize sex in, say, the porn industry (the most blatant example of "looking with intent"). But there are two problems with this.

First, when we interact with porn, we carve neural pathways. We establish a "default" response to a type of stimulus (say, women). Given the amount of dopamine (the feel-good chemical) involved, we carve very deep neural pathways. Our conscious mind may want to set boundaries on when we go down those pathways, but our unconscious mind doesn't get that memo. We are powerfully establishing our "default" mode. Anyone who thinks this isn't going to come out in undesirable ways isn't dealing in reality. We train our brain to objectify, so that's what it's going to do.

Second, interacting with pornography is, itself, a sexual experience. As a sexual experience, it is about as non-holistic as it gets. There is no human connection there. We don't know what led that lady to choose the adult entertainment industry. We don't know what being in that industry is like for her. In fact, aside from her physical appearance, everything else we think we know about her is almost certainly made up. We don't know anything about her because that's not the point. Her value is not in who she is as a person, but in what she can do for us. And the sexual experience isn't even trying to be holistic. It's entirely physical, with just enough fake emotional connection that our emotional brain will buy it.

Whether it's consensual or not, objectifying women feeds into a non-holistic view of sex. Surprisingly, if we listen closely enough, we can catch our culture bemoaning the inadequacy of non-holistic sex. In its honest moments, our culture recognizes that holistic sex is the best sex. It's weird to see psychological literature and the most knuckle-scraping corners of the "man-o-sphere" on the same page: consuming porn makes actual sex worse.[26] Beyond that, it's common for experts to point out that the best sex is in long-term, committed relationships.[27] This is a good indicator that when we make sex non-holistic, we are breaking something.

> **Consensual or not, objectifying women feeds into a non-holistic view of sex.**

Ourselves.

Here's the problem: if holistic sex integrates the different aspects of our humanity, and non-holistic sex fractures them, then non-holistic sex, pretty much by definition, makes us less than human.

In the Sermon on the Mount, Jesus cries out that the heart of God is not to objectify our sister. Why? Because in dehumanizing her, we dehumanize us all.

THINK ABOUT IT

1. In Scripture, how does God demonstrate his faithfulness?

2. A friend of mine cynically says that "love" is often just a matter of projecting your ideal onto someone else. Is this a type of objectification?

3. In researching for a movie, Tina Fey went to a woman's workshop. There, she realized that most ladies first understood themselves as women (as opposed to girls) when a guy yelled something inappropriate at them, usually from a passing car.[28] Have you ever been objectified? How did that feel?

4. What would it look like to emphasize faithfulness in your relationships?

18

How to Cut Off Your Hand

"If your right eye causes you to stumble, gouge it out and throw it away. It is better for you to lose one part of your body than for your whole body to be thrown into hell. And if your right hand causes you to stumble, cut it off and throw it away. It is better for you to lose one part of your body than for your whole body to go into hell." (Matthew 5:29–30)

B e realistic: managing our sexuality is hard. As a guy who was single, then not single, then single again, I've experienced this issue from a lot of angles. It's a tough nut to crack.

Once, I went to a men's breakfast at church where we watched a sermon on sexual purity. It was really good. The preacher mentioned a companion sermon on singleness, so I thought, "I should look that up when I get home." That afternoon, I put it on in the background while I worked on some food prep for the week.

I couldn't finish it. Halfway through, I was literally screaming at my computer. This married guy had no idea what he was talking about.

Most Christian discussions of sexual ethics are heavy on the "why" and light on the "how to." In Matthew 5:29–30, Jesus is serious about the importance of doing something. Objectification is not okay. We get that. But often my unredeemed body doesn't care. So how? How do I steer myself away from impulses toward non-holistic sex and toward living out my sexuality in a way that mirrors the faithfulness of God?

Paul seems to say that this wasn't a problem for him, but he recognized that it was for most people (1 Corinthians 7:5–7). For them, his advice was,

"Get married" (1 Corinthians 7:8–9). To which I respond, "That's great, Paul. Do you have any names or contact information?"

Being married helps, but the unmarried can't simply wait on marriage as a cure-all. They are establishing how they manage their sexuality now, while they are single. If they do get married, they will probably have a "honeymoon phase" when things are great. But that will wear off, and the habits they built as single people will continue to be their default method for managing their sexuality. We need other solutions.

Jesus' advice involves a machete.

> If your right eye causes you to stumble, gouge it out and throw it away. It is better for you to lose one part of your body than for your whole body to be thrown into hell. And if your right hand causes you to stumble, cut it off and throw it away. It is better for you to lose one part of your body than for your whole body to go into hell. (Matthew 5:29–30)

Obviously, Jesus is speaking figuratively. (Seriously, how does someone sin with *one* eye? Was the other one just not paying attention?) But figurative language doesn't diminish the force of what he's saying. What do we do to avoid sexual immorality? Jesus says, "Whatever it takes."

Jesus says to start early in the process—at "looking with intent." This is when the objectifying, mating section of our brain initially gets triggered. In the previous chapter, we looked at the possibility of dialing this down—engaging the part of the brain that can see the big picture. The key is to humanize. Focusing on faces helps. Faces are hard to depersonalize. Especially eyes. In fact, we can get pretty far in life looking people in the eyes, smiling, and saying, "Hello." That small verbal exchange does wonders to return our headspace to a human level.

I also have a phrase I repeat to myself: "She is a person, with her own hopes, fears, and dreams. And she needs Jesus, just like me." That last bit about Jesus helps. First, it's impossible to be genuinely concerned for someone's spiritual well-being and to view them as a sex object at the same time. Second, you're inviting Jesus into that moment. He'll put it right. If you do this enough, it will become a habit. You create new neural pathways so that your default response is to keep things on a human level. You train your brain to go places you want it to go.

This is helpful for dealing with the survival brain's primal focus on keeping the species alive. But, while the survival brain is interested in sex, it usually isn't in charge of it. The emotional/social brain is. That's a problem because the emotional/social brain doesn't make choices, it runs scripts. The scripts it follows are concerned with *belonging* and *status*. If our emotional brain is in charge, our sex life will rehash every dysfunctional lesson life has taught us about how to connect with someone and where we find our value.

> You train your brain to go places you want it to go.

As with the survival brain, the first step of reframing these internal dynamics is to become aware of them. To begin with, this means learning to recognize our triggers—the situations where we are most vulnerable. For me, stress and self-pity are huge triggers. If that's where my mind is, I'm in trouble.

On a more complicated level, this means unearthing all the messages you tell yourself about connection and value. This may require counseling because this stuff usually runs deep. For instance, it's appalling how many people had terrible dads. As a result, their sex lives are about self-defeating ways to either gain masculine affirmation or affirm their own masculinity. The reality is that our value and connection is in Christ, but we all need help owning that truth.

Then there's the internet—a perfect forum for intelligent people to try and reduce us to our basic drives so that we will consume their product. When it comes to porn, they don't have to try that hard. As I tell my kids, "If it's one person versus the internet, the internet almost always wins."

The worst possible strategy for dealing with the internet is to pretend that we will just exercise "self-control." We won't. In nearly every corner of the internet, people are actively, deliberately trying to trigger a "hormone dump" in our pre-conscious brain. The deeper we go into a "hormone fog," the less we have access to our agency.

We can waste time beating ourselves up about it and hoping to "do better" the next time. Or we can leverage where we are strong to support ourselves where we are weak. Exercise our agency where we can to manage circumstances where we probably can't. Ulysses had it right. Have your companions tie you to the mast before you pass the sirens.

I bought a new modem so I could run all my Wi-Fi through one of the free content-filtering Domain Name Servers (DNS) from CleanBrowsing.org. I subscribed to some accountability software and some app monitoring software. I even had a friend set the "screen time" password on my iPhone. Is this system iron-clad? Maybe not. But it creates a "speed bump" that gives me time to get myself back into the right head space.

Setting up my technology that way took time. It cost money. It made researching for the previous chapter really hard. But short of stabbing my eyes out, I'm not sure how else to take Jesus seriously.

Lastly, the single most powerful tool I've come across for managing my sexuality is confession. It's in the Bible for a reason (James 5:16; 1 John 1:9). I proactively confessed to my wife-at-the-time once, then had no sexual struggles for the last three years of our marriage and two years beyond. Confession is powerful. Hidden dynamics that seem irresistible can be overcome when they are brought into the light. Telling someone our deepest failings may feel like cutting off a hand, but it has the power to set us free.

We're not going to eliminate our sex drive. Even eunuchs experience sexual attraction.[29] At times, our brain will want to go down those pathways. Resisting does not feel natural. It means deliberately denying our brain dopamine that we know is available. In his book *Addiction and Grace*, Gerald May calls this "walking through the desert."[30]

Thankfully, we know someone who went through that desert ahead of us. Jesus was "tempted in every way, just as we are—yet he did not sin" (Hebrews 4:15). He walked that desert his entire life. In fact, Jesus is still waiting to consummate his relationship with his bride (John 14:2–3; Ephesians 5:25–27; Revelation 19:6–9).

How do we manage our sexuality appropriately? At the end of the day, a few tips and tactics aren't going to get us there. A healthy sexuality grows out of something deeper. It grows out of walking with Jesus in every area of our lives. Sexual temptation hits me the hardest when my relationship with Jesus is the weakest. The worst mistake we can make in managing our sexuality is to try to do it alone. With Jesus by our side, we don't have to.

1. Do you know someone who keeps replaying the same bad relationship with different people?

2. What messages did your family of origin teach about how to get love and/or affirmation?

3. Have you found effective ways for dealing with temptation on the internet? What are they?

4. What would it look like to manage your sexuality in dialogue with Jesus?

19

Sincerity

"Again, you have heard that it was said to the people long ago, 'Do not break your oath, but fulfill to the Lord the vows you have made.' But I tell you, do not swear an oath at all: either by heaven, for it is God's throne, or by the earth, for it is his footstool; or by Jerusalem, for it is the city of the Great King. And do not swear by your head, for you cannot make even one hair white or black. All you need to say is simply 'Yes' or 'No'; anything beyond this comes from the evil one." (Matthew 5:33–37)

I have two boys, so I know a lot about Minecraft. It's a versatile game. It can be a digital version of playing with Legos; it can be about fighting monsters, overcoming obstacles, and beating the big boss at the end; or it can be about fighting player vs. player. It's been interesting to watch my boys' playing styles evolve. Once they became teenagers, it was all about connecting with friends online, forming teams, and crafting the best gear possible so they could go fight the other team.

Except that never happened. Inevitably, someone got bored or realized the other team was way ahead, so they would decide that it was more fun to collaborate against their own friends. They became moles, waiting for the best time to stab their teammates in the back. Usually, the mole was my son. Betrayal became the game. He enjoyed the delicious feeling of saying one thing and plotting another.

Until it happened to him. Once people on his "team" stabbed him in the back, his reaction became real-world real fast. I watched him maliciously burn his own team's base to the ground, immediately log off, then go to his room to sulk. At the end of the day, if we can't take people at their word, it cuts deep.

Jesus has something to say about this in Matthew 5:33–37:

> Again, you have heard that it was said to the people long ago, "Do not break your oath, but fulfill to the Lord the vows you have made." But I tell you, do not swear an oath at all: either by heaven, for it is God's throne, or by the earth, for it is his footstool; or by Jerusalem, for it is the city of the Great King. And do not swear by your head, for you cannot make even one hair white or black. All you need to say is simply "Yes" or "No"; anything beyond this comes from the evil one.

In the second half of Matthew 5, Jesus says six times, "You have heard it said . . . But I tell you . . ." (Matthew 5:21–48). He never says that he's quoting Scripture. He's quoting proverbs that have been floating around since the time of "the ancients" (5:33). Of course, it's all based on the Old Testament. The point of the proverbs is that these folks are concerned to keep the letter of the law.

In 5:33–37, the exact letter of the law they are dancing around often gets obscured by the translations. The NIV says, "Again, you have heard that it was said to the people long ago, 'Do not break your oath, but fulfill to the Lord the vows you have made'" (Matthew 5:33). The first part of the quote in 5:33, which we could literally translate, "Don't oath-break," looks like a good summary of Numbers 30:2. The second part, which literally says, "But repay to the Lord your oaths," looks like a good summary of Deuteronomy 23:21 (mostly based on the use of the rather general word for "give back" or "repay"). Now, since Deuteronomy 23:21 talks about repaying "vows," a lot of versions (including the NIV) use "vows" in Matthew 5:33. But that's not the word Jesus uses. Jesus says "oaths." In the Old Testament, you "swear" an "oath," and these are the only two relevant words Jesus uses in this paragraph.

Jesus is talking about *oaths*.

A vow is a promise you make to *God*. An oath is something you swear to *another person*. Now, remember, Jesus is talking to a bunch of ordinary people sitting on the side of a hill. None of these people are going to take an "oath of office." Jesus isn't talking about ceremonial oaths. He's talking about everyday stuff; you borrow your neighbor's donkey and swear you'll bring it right back.

These everyday oaths were common in the ancient world. A person could swear that they would do something (Matthew 14:6–7). They could swear that a statement was true (Matthew 26:72). They could swear loyalty to someone (Nehemiah 6:18). All these oaths took a recognized form (e.g., 2 Kings 6:31): There was a core statement—the thing they were swearing to. To this, they would add a "conditional curse," which basically said, "Otherwise, may this horrible thing happen to me." Lastly, they would invoke some higher authority or sacred thing to guarantee that this curse would happen if their oath didn't pan out.

If "the ancients" are focused on keeping the letter of the law, the key word in Jesus' quote is "to the Lord." Rather than God being the one they are swearing *to*, they are swearing *on* him. God is the higher authority invoked in the oath. That leaves absolutely no wiggle room as far as the law is concerned. Leviticus 19:12 flatly says, "Do not swear falsely by my name." If you swear by God, you have to follow through. Period.

The implied exception to the popular proverb is that, if an oath invokes something other than God, then breaking that oath wouldn't violate the letter of the law. The law says you can't swear falsely on the Lord. It doesn't say you can't swear falsely on, say, heaven, or the temple, or something else. The rabbis had mixed feelings about this, but many spelled out circumstances in which oaths weren't really binding.[31]

Of course, the only reason to swear an oath on something less than God is that we want the wiggle room. We are deliberately hedging our bets. But the problem goes beyond that. Why not just make the core statement: "I'll bring your donkey right back"? Why add the oath at all? Because, while we want to hedge our bets, we want to make sure the other person doesn't. We want the other person to commit.

An oath, then, is not straightforward communication. It is manipulation. It is a way to induce the other person to do what we want without looking behind the curtain. We have information or motives we don't want them to see.

Manipulators and leaders both influence people. But good leaders respect the people they are leading. They treat them like grown-ups and communicate honestly, with *sincerity*. Sincere communication respects people and doesn't intentionally hide information or motives that might discourage the other person's cooperation.

Good leaders also communicate sincerely because they respect the other person's interests. They try, as much as possible, to make sure the actions they are advocating benefit everyone involved.

Manipulators, on the other hand, are only concerned about their own interests. They don't really care about the other person's interests. They treat people like they are cogs in their machine. Manipulators also don't care about truth. Any connection between words and reality is irrelevant. As Nietzsche put it, words are simply "a mobile army of metaphors." Manipulators say whatever they need to say to get their "win," instrumentalizing both words and people.

That's what oaths do. In our culture, we can translate "oaths" as any way we try to add an extra guarantee that what we're saying is true. Maybe it's the sociopath who peppers his speech with, "Trust me," or the sketchy character who does not hesitate to "swear to God," or the person who makes an "unsolicited promise." On the surface, all these "oaths" claim to be a guarantee of truth, but the only reason for making them is because there is reason to doubt their truth, and the oath-taker is trying to keep the other person from noticing that. A false oath isn't just untrue; it seeks to generate trust with the explicit intent of violating that trust. Oaths violate the social contract.

Oaths violate the social contract.

When words become weapons of manipulation, that which has the power to draw us together instead tears us apart. A society marked by broken trust is a society that can't function. We become mired in cynicism. We question motives. We doubt we're getting the whole story. We hold people at arm's length. If we hear from someone outside our tribe, we simply don't believe them. We ignore their words and make up stories about their motives. In other words, we end up with the civic discourse that we have right now.

This is the work of the devil (Matthew 5:37) whose very name (*diabolo*, meaning "to throw through") carries the idea of creating separation or division. The "evil one" doesn't just want to get people to do bad things; he wants to tear them apart.

Jesus seems especially upset that people keep drawing God into this mess. Here in Matthew 5:34–36 as well as in Matthew 23:16–22, he reminds the religious leaders that they are monotheists. There are no intermediate powers to swear on. Anything sacred derives its holiness from God. Any authority derives that authority from God.

God is truth. His Word corresponds to reality so strongly that it brings things into being. This whole game of "words as weapons" offends his very nature. To explicitly invoke him in it is blasphemy.

We need to seek the sincerity that mirrors God's heart. "These are the things that you shall do: Speak the truth to one another; render in your gates judgments that are true and make for peace; do not devise evil in your hearts against one another, and love no false oath, for all these things I hate, declares the Lord" (Zechariah 8:16–17, ESV).

If we want to respect words, respect people, and respect God, a simple "yes" or "no" will do.

1. How can truth unite rather than divide?

2. There is a vulnerability in being sincere. Why might people want to avoid that?

3. Has anyone ever deliberately misled you? How did that feel?

4. Whom could you be more sincere with? How do you feel about that idea?

20

Grace

"You have heard that it was said, 'Eye for eye, and tooth for tooth.' But I tell you, do not resist an evil person. If anyone slaps you on the right cheek, turn to them the other cheek also. And if anyone wants to sue you and take your shirt, hand over your coat as well. If anyone forces you to go one mile, go with them two miles. Give to the one who asks you, and do not turn away from the one who wants to borrow from you." (Matthew 5:38–42)

Our neighborhood is small. The turn at the stoplight is the only entrance. After driving past a few rows of apartments, there's a circle big enough to have two cul-de-sacs in it. We live at the end of one of those. Sometimes, it's like something out of a Norman Rockwell painting—my kids know all the other kids in the neighborhood, and they still go out to play kickball in the street.

When they were smaller, my kids also knew which "big kids" to avoid. Michael was top of the list. He wasn't a large kid, but he was wiry and had few boundaries. One summer, it seemed like Michael and his crew were always wandering around the neighborhood simply being a presence. It was aimless. They were clearly bored, so they started yelling at passing cars— running up and flipping us off as we passed by. It wasn't hard to imagine that the next step was throwing rocks. These kids were starting to mess around in the adult world, and it seemed like they needed to find out what adult consequences looked like.

Responding with consequences felt instinctive. In fact, it probably would have been fair, but would it have actually helped anyone?

Let's say I wrong you somehow. You can respond in one of two ways: (1) You can passively take it. You end up feeling like a victim, and I feel encouraged to keep doing it. Or (2) you can resist and/or try to "get even." Chances are, I would feel like this retroactively justifies my initial behavior. So then I resist and/or try to "get even" with you. We get locked in a tit-for-tat until kingdom come and trumpet sound. We could call this the "eye-for-eye, tooth-for-tooth" script. No version of this script takes us anywhere we want to go.

The saying Jesus quotes in Matthew 5:38, "Eye for eye, and tooth for tooth," occurs not once, but three times in the Old Testament (Exodus 21:23–25; Leviticus 24:19–20; Deuteronomy 19:21). Of all Jesus' quotes from the Law, this one looks the most like he's flat-out saying, "Don't do this anymore." But then, based on what he just said in Matthew 5:19, he would be "least in the kingdom of heaven." On the contrary, he prefaced this whole discussion by stating, as strongly as he could, that he is not arguing against the Law (Matthew 5:17–19).

As with every other "ancient saying" in this chapter, folks are trying to keep the letter of the law while missing the heart. In this case, they do that by invoking a principle that wasn't meant to apply to them in the first place. The original context of this saying is courts and judges (Deuteronomy 19:16–21). Partiality and favoritism were a major concern in the Old Testament legal system (cf. Deuteronomy 16:18–20). So God lays down a basic principle of justice that applies across the board: the punishment must be proportionate to the offense—no more, no less (Deuteronomy 19:21). The rabbis developed ways to quantify offenses and monetize the punishments, but the guiding principle remained.[32]

Jesus is saying that this may be a great principle for a judge, but it's a terrible way to live our lives. If we view everyday relationships through the lens of what's "fair" (and the examples he gives are all from everyday life), we won't come anywhere close to the heart of God.

In the long history of applying this paragraph, the discussion has wandered far from everyday life. We get bogged down talking about "just war" theories, about private vs. public life, about how soldiers or heads of state should apply this paragraph to their jobs. At best, this makes this paragraph largely irrelevant to my life. How often do I worry about declaring war on someone? I need to know what to do about those punk kids in my neighborhood.

At worst, we get sidetracked into looking for exceptions: "When *doesn't* this apply?" This is a terrible approach. If we want to find a way to ignore Jesus, we will. Either way, the whole discussion misses that Jesus is not giving new rules. He is pointing to God's heart.

So what is God's heart here? "Don't resist," Jesus says, or, literally, "Don't stand against" (Matthew 5:39). Insisting on what's "fair," meeting aggression with aggression, isn't the answer. On the other hand, Jesus' examples go far beyond passively giving in. They involve giving extra. This is the definition of *grace*—an undeserved gift. Each of Jesus' examples demonstrates grace:

1. 5:39—If someone slaps you, slapping back is justice. Doing nothing is giving in. Offering the other cheek is grace.
2. 5:40—Fighting to keep your shirt is justice. Letting them have it is giving in. Offering your coat is grace.
3. 5:41—Refusing to carry the occupying soldier's gear seems fair. (Rome says the soldier has a right to ask, but who cares about them?) Going the required mile is giving in. Going a second mile is grace.
4. 5:42—Keeping your stuff is fair. Lending it is giving in. Not trying to get it back is grace.

God is a God of grace.

Grace is not easy. More accurately, grace is not natural. In a way, this paragraph in the sermon is a preview of chapter 6. There, Jesus will talk a lot about where we find our value—in the opinion of others or in God (Matthew 6:1–18). In a shame and honor society, a slap in the face (5:39) is an intolerable insult. Since most people are right-handed, a slap on the right cheek is a backhanded slap. This is so insulting that the rabbis assigned it a much stiffer fine.[33] The same could be said of being conscripted to carry the soldier's gear. It's degrading. So the question is—where do I find my value? If my self-esteem is grounded in God, then an insult from someone doesn't affect my sense of self-worth. There's nothing to be avenged.

Jesus also talks a lot about where we find our security—in our possessions or in God (Matthew 6:19–34). Losing their coat was a big deal for ordinary folks in the ancient world. A coat also functioned as a person's blanket, so even if a lender took it as collateral, they couldn't keep it overnight (Exodus 22:26–27). It's not clear what a person would do without it. But Jesus says, "Do not worry" (Matthew 6:28–33). If our security is grounded in something deeper than our possessions, then losing some of them doesn't matter quite as much.

The gracious response is possible only if we are grounded in something deeper than our reputation or possessions. Grace becomes possible only when we are grounded in eternity. This grounding gives us an inner strength not dependent on the things the people of this world think they can't afford to lose. It gives us the strength not to retaliate, but to give. Grace requires inner strength. Gandhi said that a non-violent response requires a far stronger person than a violent response does.

> **Grace becomes possible only when we are grounded in eternity.**

We need to be honest that there are situations where this principle doesn't apply. In those cases, the key question is, "Where is your heart?" When it was time for me to take up all the responsibilities of a single parent, I realized that I had to drop the word "should" out of my vocabulary entirely. What was fair, what I should have to do, was irrelevant. All that mattered was what my kids needed. Beyond that, it was just a matter of what I could do or couldn't do.

This is where boundaries come in. A boundary can be an honest appraisal that I don't have any more to give. I need to say, "no." If saying "no" is uncomfortable—if saying no feels like going against what Jesus says here—that's a good sign that our heart is in the right place. As Bonhoeffer puts it, we should always suspect that we might be better off if we followed Jesus in "single-minded obedience."[34]

But sometimes grace compels us to say "no." Grace wants to help, but if someone is asking for something harmful, there isn't any grace in giving it. (It is not an act of grace, for example, to enable an abuser.)

What if the opposite of "standing against" isn't "giving in"? What if the opposite of "standing against" is "coming alongside"? Instead of asking, "What is the fair response to the aggressor?" we ask, "How can I help this person?" This is tricky for the person who slaps you. But if this "slap" is primarily an insult, it looks a lot like what I often see working in retail.

Almost every day, someone takes their particular inconvenience as a reason to insult the workers helping them. The response could be, "You need to vent? That's fine. I won't take it personally. When you're done, we'll see what we can figure out."

It's more straightforward in the other cases: "You need clothes? Here, take it all." Or, "You need to get your gear all the way to Sepphoris? Here, I can go with you a little farther." Or, "You need to borrow something? Here, just take it."

That is not how the "eye-for-eye, tooth-for-tooth" script is supposed to go. "Coming alongside" is not one of the options. That's the strength required by grace—the strength to act from your internal convictions. It's the strength to live out a different script.

Flipping the script is not intuitive for anyone involved. You can see this in the other person's confused face. They are disoriented because they thought this was an adversarial encounter. But with a "grace" script, you are on the same team. (In fact, it's helpful to use the words "we" and "us" to signal that you are now in this together.)

Gandhi said that the non-violent response is effective when the goal is to win the other person over. "Don't resist" leads into "love your enemy" in the next paragraph (Matthew 5:43–48). In fact, Luke scrambles the two paragraphs together (Luke 6:27–36).

I could have given those neighborhood kids a long, angry honk. I could have stopped the car and chewed them out. I could have even called the authorities. Instead, I treated them like what they were—neighbors. When I passed, before they could flip me off, I smiled and waved. After only a couple times, Michael found himself waving back. As Paul says, "Do not be overcome by evil, but overcome evil with good" (Romans 12:17–21).

There's no guarantee that this will always work. Maybe that's one reason Jesus puts no emphasis on the other person's reaction. You don't control them. You control you. You are in charge of the direction you take your heart.

It's your choice: Will you have a heart that is locked in the cycle of "justice," or a heart freed by grace?

THINK ABOUT IT

1. Grace is giving extra in order to help. In what ways does God do this?

2. Why is it so common to "stand against" rather than "come alongside"?

3. Have you ever returned "an eye for an eye"? How did that work?

4. Is there someone you need to try a "grace approach" with?

21

Persecutors

"Love your enemies and pray for those who persecute you." (Matthew 5:43)

Amid months of protests in Portland, Oregon, Bibles were burned in August 2020. The *Washington Examiner* first reported on videos of small bonfires that surfaced on Twitter.[35] Fact checkers swooped in to confirm that, yes, this happened.[36] Conservative commentators saw this as part of a larger pattern of Christianity coming under attack in America. The Portland Bible burning was "exhibit #1" for one columnist who wrote, "With violence in the streets of many of our most prominent cities, there is an underlying subtheme that is also troubling. Christophobia, which attacks anything Christian, is surely on the march."[37] For decades in America, persecution seemed like something from ancient stories or far off places. Now, it's back in the headlines.

After discussing persecution in the Beatitudes, Jesus returns to the theme in Matthew 5:44. What, exactly, is persecution? The New Testament uses the word without ever defining it. While United States' immigration law never defines it either, case law dealing with asylum seekers over the years paints a picture: Persecution is more than mere harassment, but it is not limited to physical harm. It can take the form of physical violence, torture, or other violations of human rights; threats of harm; unlawful detention; infliction of mental, emotional, or psychological harm; or even substantial economic discrimination or harm.[38]

More important than the *what* of persecution is the *why*: Why does persecution happen? When Christians are persecuted for their faith, it's easy to assume that the persecutors are simply evil people who hate God. But if we look at persecution in general, we find that it is often far more complicated and, unfortunately, far more human.

In their book *Why Not Kill Them All?*, Chirot and McCauley look at the conditions that lead to genocide.[39] Since genocide is the most extreme form of persecution, their observations can tell us a lot about why persecution happens. Certain psychological conditions have to exist for a person to engage in persecution. We could call this "the path to becoming a persecutor."

First, view people collectively, not individually. Individuals are unique and complicated. Our conscious mind can only handle so much at one time, so it is always looking for patterns—ways to simplify and categorize things. Including people. It's hard to avoid doing this, but it is the first step to viewing someone as less than fully human. The only way to make people fit into groups is to shave off some of those complicated bits that make them who they are.

Second, draw a line separating "us" from "them." This group we just formed in our minds is not *our* group; they are "other." We can draw this line on the basis of race, religion, nationality, political opinion, membership in some social group, etc. It doesn't matter what the line is; what matters is how sharply we draw it. (Of course, these lines are always much fuzzier than we pretend they are.)

In and of itself, making distinctions isn't bad. Just because I'm a Gen-Xer and you're a Millennial doesn't mean we're going to war. Social scientists constantly draw lines like this. But again, this is another necessary step on the path.

Third, we essentialize people based on this difference. Whatever distinguishes their group from ours isn't viewed merely as a fact *about* them. It's not just one of many characteristics we could have chosen for our Venn diagram. Rather, we believe that this characteristic captures their essence. It's who they *are*. We reduce them to that one characteristic.

Fourth, we decide that this difference between "us" and "them" is fundamentally bad. This is the most extreme version of "othering." This is hatred. Hatred is the perception of a negative essence. It says that this characteristic that captures the essence of who they are is evil. And if they're evil, then the gloves are off. In the battle between good and evil, there are no holds barred. We can now justify any measure we take against them.

Fifth, add enough fear, and we feel obligated to take action against them. When fear enters the picture, the other group is perceived as a threat. This threat must be answered, especially if it feels like their existence threatens ours.

It might not seem like anyone would ever see Christians as an existential threat, but people often do. For example:

- Since Christians acknowledge a higher allegiance than the state, a totalitarian regime like China doesn't feel that it can count on their loyalty.
- A Hindu community in India may define themselves by their religious purity. When a group fears that its purity is threatened, things can get especially nasty. Christians, simply by existing, threaten that purity.
- Groups like Columbian Marxist rebels need a flow of new recruits to survive. They won't get any from a village where the Christian message has taken root.

In all these cases, Christians can be seen as a threat simply for living out their faith in Jesus.

And finally, power. If we check off all these boxes—we see individuals as part of a group, that group as different than ours, that difference as essential and fundamentally bad, and that group as a threat—then the only missing ingredient is *power*. Given enough power, persecution will occur. It's not always the state that persecutes. If the state either doesn't care what a group does or isn't strong enough to stop them, then it's not hard for that group to persecute.

If someone objects to something these persecutors do, no matter how horrifying it may seem, they respond, "You don't understand. These are evil people who hate everything good."

If you've ever thought this about a persecutor, then the two of you have something in common, after all. This "path to persecution" is not unique to some special kind of monster. The instinctive attitude we can have *toward* a persecutor is the exact attitude that can turn us *into* a persecutor.

We see this "path to persecution" playing out in our culture—essentializing, hatred, fear. To what extent will these psychological conditions find a home in the American church? As I write this, I have an ominous sense that this is exactly the devil's plan. A couple of people burn a few Bibles in a country where 20 million copies are sold every year,[40] and this is painted as an existential threat.

That fear could fuel, say, some Christian Nationalist movement that blurs the distinction between Jesus' Kingdom and the United States. They could use political power and control to try to eliminate whatever they feel threatens them.

But in doing so, they would profane everything Christ stands for. Therefore, other Christians could see them as the danger, and fight against them accordingly. While the Right and the Left claim to be opposites, this fear-fueled power struggle for the very existence of the good blinds everyone into walking down the exact same path—the path of the persecutor.

Jesus calls his people to walk back from the brink.

Jesus calls his people to walk back from the brink.

- Away from *power*. Jesus praises meekness (Matthew 5:5). Power is not the weapon his people use (Matthew 26:52; John 18:36).
- Away from *fear*. Chapter 6 will remind us that our treasure is in heaven. There's nothing we value that the world can take away.
- Away from *hatred*. Jesus urges mercy (Matthew 5:7) and love (Matthew 5:44).
- Finally, nearly every paragraph here at the end of Matthew 5 is about *humanizing* people—about not reducing their unique, God-given individuality and dignity. Whom are you afraid of? Ask Jesus how you can humanize them.

Prayer is a powerful tool for doing this. Not just prayer about them. Jesus says to pray for them, "Love your enemies and pray for those who persecute you" (Matthew 5:44). When Andrew Brunson spent two years in prison in Turkey for his faith, the prayer he developed for his persecutors was that God's Kingdom and blessing would come to them.[41] I've found that Jesus' prayer from the cross is also powerful: "Father, forgive them, for they don't know what they're doing" (Luke 23:34). This is God's heart, both for the ones we "other" and the ones who "other" us. In praying for them, we invite God to make his heart for them our heart for them.

Instead of walking the path of dehumanization, hatred, and fear, I can choose to walk Jesus' path. Jesus' path means losing the world, but it also means saving my soul. His path won't keep me from encountering a persecutor, but it will keep me from becoming one.

THINK ABOUT IT

1. Paul was a persecutor-turned-missionary. What does that say about persecutors?

2. Jesus says to pray for our persecutors. How could you do this?

3. Do you recognize yourself in any of these "steps" in the path to becoming a persecutor? Do you recognize any of them in your community?

4. How does focusing on the Kingdom keep someone from becoming a persecutor?

22

Love

"You have heard that it was said, 'Love your neighbor and hate your enemy.' But I tell you, love your enemies and pray for those who persecute you, that you may be children of your Father in heaven. He causes his sun to rise on the evil and the good, and sends rain on the righteous and the unrighteous. If you love those who love you, what reward will you get? Are not even the tax collectors doing that? And if you greet only your own people, what are you doing more than others? Do not even pagans do that? Be perfect, therefore, as your heavenly Father is perfect." (Matthew 5:43–48)

One of my best friends in college had a colorful past. He was ex-military and spent time as a genuine street thug. In fact, he was high on cocaine when he responded to an altar call. But God calls whom he wants, so there my friend was in Bible college.

My senior year was 2001. The morning of September 11, I was heading to a corner room in the chapel to take a Church History test. But, as I passed the tech room, I saw people watching live TV. A skyscraper was burning somewhere.

That evening, the dorm lobby was full. We were sitting and standing, frozen in front of the TV and asking questions we couldn't even articulate.

But not my friend. He was pacing back and forth near the door, incapable of inaction. It was a side of him I knew was there but had never seen before. He wanted someone to kill.

That sentiment stuck around for a lot of people. A minister told me about a person he knew who kept a picture of Osama bin Laden on his dartboard. When it came to that man, nothing seemed more natural—morally necessary, even—than to "hate your enemies."

Jesus' last quote from "the ancients" is, "You have heard that it was said, 'Love your neighbor and hate your enemy'" (Matthew 5:43). If the purpose of the Old Testament law was to reveal God's heart, there's probably no command that does this more directly than, "Love your neighbor as yourself" (Leviticus 19:18). How do we avoid God's heart on this one? Easy: make our "neighbor" the *only* one we need to love. "Sure, I'll love my neighbor. But the second he crosses me, he's not my neighbor anymore, so forget that guy." People wanted this loophole so badly that they made it *part of the proverb*: "and hate your enemy."

No rabbi sanctioned hating your enemies.[42] This was street-level stuff. "Enemy" is a visceral, emotional word. Somebody hates somebody. Even if you don't hate them, they hate you. Hating them back is the natural response. Loving my neighbor is fine, but of course I'm going to hate my enemies. That's what you do.

But that's not what God does. Nowhere else in the Sermon on the Mount is Jesus so clearly calling people to the heart of God. He wants us to become "children of your Father in heaven" (Matthew 5:45), mirroring his character. And there is nothing more central to God's character than love. If we're going to understand what Jesus is calling us to, then we have to understand the word "love."

We can start with the point everyone makes (and rightly so): Love, particularly *agape* (the word used in Matthew 5:43–48), is more than a feeling. Love does things (1 John 3:18). Specifically, love involves *selfless action*. Love costs something. According to Jesus, the greater the cost, the greater the love (John 15:13). M. Scott Peck's definition of "love" (slightly paraphrased) is "the willingness to extend one's self for one's own or another's spiritual growth."[43] I like this definition because it distinguishes love from, say, codependence, which doesn't benefit anyone.

True, love is not *just* an emotion. But sometimes it seems like theologians want to cut the emotion out of *agape* altogether. Good luck with that. Next time you tell your spouse, "I love you," try substituting that with, "I am mechanically committed to your well-being."

There goes date night.

This is simply not how the word is used—neither the English word "love" nor the Greek word *agape*. To understand the word, we need to be clear about how love actually works. We could call this the "structure" of love.

First, we perceive some *positive characteristic* of the thing loved. As a result, we feel good about that thing. For simplicity's sake, we'll call this emotion "affection." If this is as far as we get—a positive characteristic that generates affection—that's *eros*, which is more like "desire" or "enjoyment."

Now, if we have one foot on "positive characteristic" and the other on "affection," the more we shift our weight toward affection, the more we're looking at *philos*. This is a common word for love. The noun is actually the word for "friend." It implies a lot of affection, and not much else.

Action takes us a step further in this structure. *Agape* puts one foot on affection and the other on *selfless action*. Yes, *agape* emphasizes selfless action, but it never takes its foot off of affection. In fact, the word is comfortable putting all of its weight there. Thus, people can have *agape* toward things—like Pharisees who love the good seats (Luke 11:43) or Demas, who loved the present age (2 Timothy 4:10). Likewise, *agape* is sometimes synonymous with the very emotional *philos* (compare John 11:3 to 11:5 and 20:2 to 21:20). Sometimes *agape* clearly emphasizes affection (Mark 10:21; Luke 7:41–47; 1 Peter 1:22). There are, in fact, no verses in which *agape* clearly excludes affection. Affection is always present, at least on the periphery. *Agape* simply means "affection that generates selfless action." If we don't want to imply affection, we use a different word—like "duty" or "service."

This definition of love as "affection that generates selfless action" fits how the word is actually used, but it raises some problems.

First, our feelings, including affection, come and go. They make for an unstable foundation. So, to make a serious relationship work, this "selfless action" must become a *commitment*. The purpose of this commitment is to sustain the selfless action even when we're not "feeling it." This is a good thing. It is a virtue. (Some writers take this to be the exact meaning of *storge*).

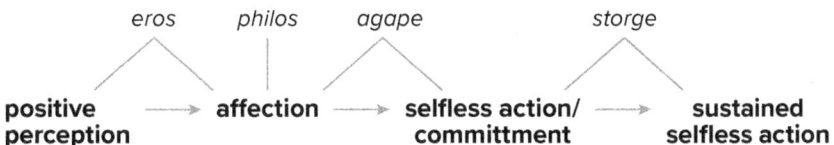

eros	philos	agape		storge
positive perception →	**affection** →	**selfless action/ committment** →		**sustained selfless action**

This is a practical reality of being human, but it leads some theologians to say that love *is* "selfless action generated by a commitment." This may be the best we humans can do but (a) it ignores most of the ways the word is used and (b) it cannot be true of God.

God's love is not generated by anything prior to it—commitment or otherwise. It's not the outcome of some more fundamental characteristic of God. It is his essence. As an eternally existing Trinity, God is love (1 John 4:8, 16). As humans, we can't ground our love in feelings because our feelings come and go. When my internal resources are depleted, there goes my compassion. God doesn't have that problem. His internal resources are infinite. His affection is eternal, un-generated. For God, love comes first.

His affection is eternal, un-generated. For God, love comes first.

This does something interesting to the structure of love. The statement "I love you" usually includes the beginning of the diagram. It often means, "I perceive something lovable in you." But how could it mean this for God if God's love is not based on any prior condition? Unlike *eros*, where affection is the response to the lovable quality, God's *agape* works backward. Our lovableness is a result of his affection. His love *makes* us lovable. I am lovable because I am loved by him.

God's agape

positive characteristic ←——— affection ———→ selfless action

So there is no reason to exclude emotion from God's love. In fact, if we remove the affection from love, we will never grasp "how wide and long and high and deep is the love of Christ" (Ephesians 3:18). It's one thing to say that God is mechanically committed to our well-being. It is infinitely more powerful to say that God actually *loves* us.

Even those who hate him. John 3:16 says, "God so loved the world" (John's shorthand for the forces that are opposed to God). Romans 5:8 says, "God demonstrated his own love for us in this: While we were still sinners, Christ died for us." Our actions are powerless to blunt his affection. No,

God doesn't love everything we do, but he sees past our sin to our core self that is created in his image. God's love is more like a parent who says to their child, "I know you're broken, but you're still precious to me." And so he gives sun and rain to us all (Matthew 5:45).

This is the love Jesus calls us to—love that is not contingent and therefore is not limited. Not love that is *reciprocal*—that loves only those who love us (Matthew 5:46). Not love that is *tribal*—that only loves our brothers (Matthew 5:47). But love that is *universal*, complete. Or, as the Greeks would put it, love that is "perfect" (Matthew 5:48).

This love is *the* command. "My command is this: Love each other as I have loved you" (John 15:12; 2 John 6). This love is everything the law was trying to do (Romans 13:8–10; Galatians 5:14; James 2:8). As Christians, we are grounded in this love (Ephesians 3:17), and it is the context in which we do everything else (1 Corinthians 14:1; 16:14; Galatians 5:6). If we don't have it, we have nothing (1 Corinthians 13:1–3).

The second problem theologians have with defining love as "affection that generates selfless action" is that we can't command our feelings. But this forgets the whole point of Matthew chapter 5: the Kingdom of God is not about rules. It's about taking on the heart of God.

Even so, this is too much. Maybe God has un-generated affection even for those who hate him, but I don't. For me to love in this way—to have affection for my enemies—would take an honest-to-goodness miracle. Our culture's sentimentalized "be the miracle" nonsense won't do. God has to actually intervene in human history and give me his heart.

This is exactly how Richard Wurmbrand processed his experience at the hands of his Communist torturers. In the midst of horrifying pain and brutality, a miracle occurred. He suddenly started seeing his torturers through God's eyes. He saw the humanity in the people who were breaking his body. And they were beautiful. This was not from him, and he knew it:

> I have seen Christians in Communist prisons with fifty pounds of chains on their feet, tortured with red-hot iron pokers, in whose throats spoonfuls of salt had been forced, being kept afterwards without water, starving, whipped, suffering from cold—and praying with fervor for the Communists. This is humanly inexplicable! It is the love of Christ, which was poured out in our hearts.[44]

Jesus wasn't kidding. "I am the vine; you are the branches. If you remain in me and I in you, you will bear much fruit; apart from me you can do nothing" (John 15:5). And what is this fruit? The next paragraph is an extended discussion about love. By the end, it's clear: love is both command and fruit (John 15:16–17). All we do—all we can do—is remain in him. There's no telling how long it will take and what Jesus will need to do in us to get us there. But if we are to love as he loved, we must abide and God must act. There is no other way.

THINK ABOUT IT

1. Loving the sinner in spite of the sin is complicated. Setting aside issues of forgiveness and reconciliation for a later chapter, how can we see the person who wronged us through God's eyes?

2. In what circumstances does your love tend to "run out"?

3. Jesus says that God shows his love though his actions (e.g., sending rain and sun). How could you do the same?

4. God loves you. Sit with that. What is your honest emotional response?

23

In Secret

*"Be careful not to practice your righteousness in
front of others to be seen by them. If you do, you will
have no reward from your Father in heaven.
"So when you give to the needy, do not announce it with
trumpets, as the hypocrites do in the synagogues and on
the streets, to be honored by others. Truly I tell you, they
have received their reward in full. But when you give to the
needy, do not let your left hand know what your right hand
is doing, so that your giving may be in secret. Then your
Father, who sees what is done in secret, will reward you.
"And when you pray, do not be like the hypocrites, for they love
to pray standing in the synagogues and on the street corners
to be seen by others. Truly I tell you, they have received their
reward in full. But when you pray, go into your room, close
the door and pray to your Father who is unseen. Then your
Father, who sees what is done in secret, will reward you. . . .
"And when you fast, do not look somber as the hypocrites do,
for they disfigure their faces to show others they are fasting.
Truly I tell you, they have received their reward in full. But when
you fast, put oil on your head and wash your face, so that it
will not be obvious to others that you are fasting, but only to
your Father, who is unseen; and your Father, who sees what
is done in secret, will reward you."* (Matthew 6:1–6, 16–18)

The Soviet gulag system seemed designed to corrupt people. Aleksandr Solzhenitsyn watched respectable men of high ideals transform into feral creatures prepared to betray everyone around them to survive. The "camp philosophy" was, "You die first and I'll die later."[45] The true "son of Gulag" was characterized by "the drive for life, pitilessness, resourcefulness, secretiveness, and mistrustfulness."[46]

Since the only faith allowed in the Soviet Union was faith in the inevitable class triumph, Christians were constantly among the millions poured into the camp system. Solzhenitsyn watched Christians get sifted into two groups—those who stayed faithful and those who did not.

> There was a multitude of Christians: prisoner transports and graveyards, prisoner transports and graveyards. Who will count those millions? They died unknown, casting only in their immediate vicinity a light like a candle. They were the best of Russia's Christians. The worst had all . . . trembled, recanted, and gone into hiding.[47]

Uspensky was one of the worst examples. A priest who was the son of a priest, he knew he had a target on his back. His strategy for taking it off was to murder his own father as an act of "class hatred." After a light sentence, he became an important official in gulag. Christians like him had a Christianity dependent on the external institution. When it collapsed, so did they.

Yet Solzhenitsyn had to account for the throngs of Christians who did not recant and were not broken by the system. "They went off to camp to face tortures and death—only so as not to renounce their faith! They knew very well *for what* they were serving time, and they were unwavering in their convictions! They were the only ones, perhaps, to whom the camp philosophy and even the camp language did not stick."[48] "They died—most certainly, but . . . they were not corrupted."[49] His conclusion for how people kept their souls intact in gulag was that they were grounded by something in their core: "No camp can corrupt those who have a stable nucleus."[50]

M. Scott Peck outlines four stages in a person's spiritual development.[51] The first is *chaos*. A person is unregulated—internally or externally. Think of someone like a rebellious teenager or a drug addict. The second is *institution*. Some external organization—like school, the military, or maybe church—steps in to provide structure from the outside. The more a person internalizes this structure, the less they depend on the institution. So they become *critical*—pointing out the flaws in the institution, perhaps leaving it altogether. Although this internalized structure can help them lead functional lives (sometimes spectacularly so), there still is a transcendent reality that calls to them. They can choose to respond to this from a more personal, *mystical* place. Peck notes that every major religion is a major religion precisely because it can function on both the institutional and mystical levels.

Like a good psychiatrist, Peck doesn't say that any one stage is better than the others. They are all just places where people might find themselves on a particular path.

I'm not sure Jesus would agree.

If the second half of Matthew 5 is an exploration of God's heart, Matthew 6 is an exploration of *my* heart. Where is my heart? In Matthew 6:1–6, 16–18, Jesus talks about "hypocrites" (elsewhere, he makes it clear that he's still talking about the scribes and Pharisees; see Matthew 23:13). The term "hypocrite" comes from the Greek theater—something any decent-sized Graeco-Roman town had. The hypocrites were the actors. If the actors put on a good show, they got their applause, and that was it. Everyone went home (Matthew 6:2, 5, 16).

Greek actors held masks over their faces to indicate what role they were playing. So, for a hypocrite, there is always a disconnect between the mask and the person underneath. The external and internal are totally different stories.

For the hypocrites in Matthew 6, the disconnect in the actor is revealed by a disconnect in the *audience.* The purpose of a religious practice is, ostensibly, to connect with God. But all the practices Jesus mentions in Matthew 6 also have potential for a human audience. Throw your money in the temple jar just right, and you could make a substantial racket. Make sure you're in a good crowd at the regular times for prayer (cf. Acts 3:1), and plenty of people will notice. Everyone knows that serious religious people skip breakfast and lunch on Mondays and Thursdays (Luke 18:11–12; Mark 2:18)—not to mention the Day of Atonement (Leviticus 16:29–31)! Make sure to look extra miserable.

But why would someone do that? If the purpose of a religious act is to connect with God, why would someone make it a show for other people, instead? Because they never moved beyond the trappings of the institution to an internalized, heart connection. They are functioning on an institutional level and have never actually met God at the mystical, personal level.

When religious acts don't have anything to do with God, they perform a purely social function. They are done *for the purpose of* being seen by others (Matthew 6:1). Maybe, like the ancient Pharisees or the occasional modern politician, their purpose is to gain status within a group. Or maybe, like with most folks, religious acts are just a way to signal belonging. The show demonstrates their credentials as a card-carrying member of the group. Nowadays, we call this "virtue signaling"—putting on some little display that doesn't cost us much but that also doesn't accomplish anything other than showing that we share the values of the group.

But wait. In this very Gospel, Jesus anticipates public gatherings of believers (Matthew 18:15–20). Corporate worship is important (Hebrews 10:25), which means that we will do religious things around other people. So we have a dilemma. Is it a show or not? How can we discern true devotion from a well-constructed performance?

It's a matter of the heart. So, when it comes to other people, we usually can't. "People look at the outward appearance, but the LORD looks at the heart" (1 Samuel 16:7).

Maybe that's why, while Jesus uses the plural "you" in most of the Sermon on the Mount, he switches to the singular in 6:1–6, 16–18. Each of us must ask, "Is *my* faith expression sincere?" To determine that, Jesus proposes a thought experiment:

Think of any religious activity you engage in.

Now, take all the people away.

Does anything change in what the practice means?

Does anything change in your motivation to do it?

This may be challenging for us. It was mind-blowing in Jesus' day. People processed life on a communal level. If Jesus hadn't clearly been saying that his disciples' most important faith expressions were done in secret, no sociologist would believe that anyone in the ancient world could think like this.

But that's how Jesus challenges us to think.

This "thought experiment" is a reality in places where Christians face strong persecution. They have to practice their faith in secret. Their only rational options are authentic faith or no faith.

In the United States, this thought experiment became an actual social experiment during the pandemic. We were explicitly asked to perform our religious acts in secret. As Francis Chan urged, we could have taken this as an opportunity to examine our faith and ground it even more deeply in our heart.

Some did. Some didn't.

But if our faith practice doesn't come from the heart, it's more like a religious-looking form of "practical atheism." "Practical atheism" is claiming to believe in God but functioning like someone who doesn't. True atheism was almost unheard of in the ancient world. Even today, around 80 percent of Americans say that they believe in God. This "belief" just makes little or no difference in most of their lives.

External religious performance is not the difference Jesus is looking for. It doesn't say anything about a person's actual belief in God. The Pharisees demonstrate that "practical atheism" can be alive and well even in someone who puts on a spectacular religious show. What happens if their audience is taken away? Their theism vanishes like smoke.

On the other hand, hidden religious actions do say something about how genuine a person's faith is. Performing religious deeds in secret only makes sense if you believe God is real and you find value in your relationship with him apart from any benefit this world can provide.

> **Hidden religious actions do say something about how genuine a person's faith is.**

A good way to make sure you have faith that is rooted in your heart is to start with exactly what Jesus says. Practice some spiritual disciplines. Alone. Put priority on the relationship between you and your heavenly Father. Ground your faith there (Luke 5:16). Giving, praying, and fasting are a great start, but there are many other disciplines for cultivating your inner connection to God.[52]

From that internal foundation, you can safely take your faith public, because you're not concerned with what people see or don't see. It's not about them.

Phyllis Tickle literally wrote the modern-day book on regular, timed prayer.[53] Once, she was in a store with a friend when her alarm went off.[54] It was time to pray. Her friend was mortified. Public prayer may have earned someone street-cred in first-century Palestine, but it doesn't in a twenty-first-century place of business. Phyllis didn't pray because of the people around her; she prayed in spite of them. Her faith practice flowed from her heart, so the presence or absence of people was irrelevant.

Why? Because no one aside from God can see your heart. Therefore, whatever you do in your heart is, in fact, something done in secret. The One who sees the heart sees that you are offering your heart to him. And your heavenly Father, who sees what is done in secret, will reward you.

THINK ABOUT IT

1. If you saw the Pharisees' religious performance, how would you react? What would be your emotional response? Why?

2. An earlier chapter briefly mentions the possibility of using Christianity as "a convenient framework for constructing our cultural identity." What does this mean? Where do you see this at work?

3. Do you engage in any modern-day forms of Christian "virtue signaling"? What are they? Could you ground these in an inner connection to God? If so, how?

4. How is your private life with God? What could you do to strengthen it?

24

Kingdom Come

"And when you pray, do not keep on babbling like pagans, for they think they will be heard because of their many words. Do not be like them, for your Father knows what you need before you ask him. This, then, is how you should pray: Our Father in heaven, hallowed be your name, your kingdom come, your will be done, on earth as it is in heaven." (Matthew 6:7–10)

W hy would you pray for God's Kingdom to come when you could stick a knife in a Roman's neck instead? That's what the Jewish Sicarii did. They would go to large public gatherings dressed in ordinary, inconspicuous clothes. After working their way next to their target, they would discreetly stab them, then blend into the crowd undetected. The people in the crowd had no idea until suddenly some Roman sympathizer slumped to the ground in a pool of his own blood. The Pharisees could pray all they wanted. The Sicarii were *doing* something.

Changing the world for the better is tricky business. Susan Neiman observes that those who try to improve the world through force "usually do more harm than they set out to prevent."[55] The Sicarii hardly demonstrate otherwise. Under siege by the Romans, a large group of them eventually committed mass suicide at Masada in AD 73. These and other armed revolts eventually resulted in the Romans deporting nearly all Jewish people from the region. It would be hundreds of years before they could return.

If force is a losing strategy, then what is the alternative? Prayer involves the admission that we don't know. When Jesus teaches his disciples to pray in Matthew 6:7–15, his prayer begins by taking a posture of humility before

God: "Our Father in heaven, hallowed be your name, your kingdom come, your will be done, on earth as it is in heaven" (Matthew 6:9–10).

The hypocrites' intent in their religious practice was to manipulate people. Jesus tells us not to do that (Matthew 6:1–6, 16–18). But he also wants us to avoid the pagan mindset of thinking that we can manipulate God (6:7–8). The pagan gods were capricious and, if you buttered them up enough, very manipulable. Of course, you can't manipulate God. But Jesus also wants us to realize that we don't need to. God is a loving Father who values us (6:26), knows what we need (6:8), and will take care of us (7:11).

When this truth takes hold of us, prayer becomes something fundamentally different. As a preacher from a bygone era put it, "Prayer is more an atmosphere than an act, more an attitude than a deed, more a spirit than doing something."[56] Yes, we still pray for the things we need (6:11), but the asking has more to do with a relationship than with a transaction (7:7–11). In *The Magician's Nephew*, Aslan knew, of course, that Digory and his friends would need food for their journey. "But," says the flying horse, "I've sort of an idea that he likes to be asked."[57] Asking for stuff is not about informing God. It is about taking the right posture in relationship to him.

This posture of humility begins by recognizing his holiness: Matthew 6:9 literally says, "May your name be holy." To be "holy" is to be separate—above and apart from. God is truly "other." He is the Creator, and we are the creation. "As the heavens are higher than the earth, so are my ways higher than your ways and my thoughts than your thoughts" (Isaiah 55:9). Prayer is not about trying to get God to line up with our interests; it's about getting us to line up with his. We put our basic human needs—both social (6:1–18) and physical (6:24–34)—in the back seat so we can seek the Kingdom first (6:33).

But does praying, "Your kingdom come," actually constitute doing anything? That partly depends on when the Kingdom comes. If it only comes later, then all we can do is sit and wait. This question triggers the anthill of millennial theories. Millennial theories tend to get lost in the weeds, but they fundamentally ask *when* the Kingdom comes in relation to Jesus' return. Premillennialism says that Jesus returns before the Kingdom comes. Postmillennialism says he returns after. Amillennialism says that it's both.

Premillennialism is correct that the Kingdom won't be fully realized until Jesus comes back. That is when God's dwelling place will be among people (Revelation 21:3). That is when "there will be no more death or mourning or crying or pain" (Revelation 21:4). On the other hand, amillennialism is correct that the Kingdom has already started breaking in. In the work of Christ, the Kingdom has "come near" (Matthew 4:17). On the third hand, postmillennialism is correct that the Kingdom can be progressively realized here on earth. This is what we pray for—that God will reach down into this broken world and make something right. When he does, his Kingdom has come just a little bit more.

So, yes, the Kingdom can come. And we're not just spectators when it does. We partner with God in the realization of the Kingdom. Prayer is one way we do that. We help make things better when we reorient ourselves to seek his Kingdom his way.

So what is his way? In Romans 8, Paul strongly indicates that the redemption of creation begins with our redemption: "For the creation waits in eager expectation for the children of God to be revealed" (Romans 8:19). The Sermon on the Mount *is* Jesus' strategy for how the Kingdom comes on earth. As we are personally transformed to live out Kingdom values, we partner with God in making that Kingdom a reality in the world around us.

We partner with God in the realization of the Kingdom.

We cannot skip this step. We cannot implement the Kingdom "out there" without first implementing it "in here." The Kingdom works from the inside out. Get this wrong (as so many "Christian" efforts have in the past), and we don't produce the Kingdom. We produce some theocratic dystopia that may vaguely resemble a "lamb," but is marked by pride and blasphemy (Revelation 13:1–2, 5, 11). We do more harm than we set out to prevent. No Christian should ever be confused by the question, "Do the ends justify the means?" The answer is *no*. "What good will it be for someone to gain the whole world yet forfeit their soul?" (Matthew 16:26). If we're not doing it God's way, we're not truly seeking God's will.

This world is broken. Scripture is the story of God's work to fix it. Healing comes to the world as we submit ourselves to a holy God, setting our will and our kingdoms aside for his. This posture of prayer is, in fact, the most powerful thing we can do to change the world.

THINK ABOUT IT

1. Can you think of times in history when people tried to bring about God's Kingdom by force? How did that work out?

2. How is prayer an act of humility?

3. How is prayer an act of seeking the Kingdom first?

4. How would this "posture of humility" reorient your perspective on life?

25

Daily Bread

"Give us today our daily bread." (Matthew 6:11)

A prayer for "daily bread" (Matthew 6:11) lands differently in different places.

Take my friends in southern Kenya. We knew the drought there was bad. It was big enough that we could find news online, but we didn't need to. Folks were sending us pictures of dry riverbeds and barren ground that should have been knee-high grass. The Maasai are traditionally cattle herders. Nowadays, most folks have a side job—a dirt bike that serves as a taxi or a small shop in town—but people still see raising livestock as the ideal way to make a living. Goats are basically cash, and cows are a person's retirement and emergency savings. More than that, though, they know their cows better than most Westerners know their pets.

The drought went on long enough that the messages expressed concern with how they were going to feed their people. The rain came in time for them, but for the animals, it was too late. One well-off family sent their cows to Tanzania where there was still grass. Most people couldn't afford that. When I got to Kenya, Francis showed me a picture of his last cow. Rather, it was a picture of him pulling a plastic bag out of his last cow's stomach. That was the final thing it tried to eat before it died.

Thinking about the differences between my life and the lives of my friends in Kenya prompts serious soul searching about what this prayer means.

Jesus tells us to pray for our "daily bread" (Matthew 6:11). We don't know exactly what the word for "daily" means. It's not used anywhere but here and in Luke's version of the Lord's Prayer (Luke 11:3). (Some second century church fathers who spoke Greek thought the Gospel writers just made it up!) But, a few verses later, Jesus will talk about literal, physical bread. Matthew says to give us this bread "today," and Luke says, "each day." So there's no need to get fancy with it. It's the stuff we physically need for the present moment.

Looking at this from my standpoint in America, even as someone who receives government aid, I'm not sure whether to laugh or throw up. Having been in a "house" that was built by hand from a mixture of dirt and cow dung, I can't avoid the reality that I, like most Americans, am stupidly, obscenely rich. How can affluent Westerners possibly pray this prayer with a straight face? Or with any integrity?

First, I could take "bread" metaphorically. Even if food usually isn't a problem for me, each day still has enough troubles of its own (Matthew 6:34). When life gets overwhelming, I can still pray this prayer as a prayer of *dependence*. I recognize that the only way I'm going to make it is with God's help. The good news is that nothing is too big for God, but nothing is too small for him either. If "daily bread" makes it into the Lord's Prayer, then God is not indifferent to this little moment that seems so overwhelming to me. I can bring it to him to help me through it. I often paraphrase this prayer, "Give me the strength to make it through today." (I call this the "parents' prayer.")

Even if I return my focus to my material needs, I can still pray this prayer as a prayer of *gratitude*. When God was about to lead his people into the promised land, his advice was not that they shouldn't live comfortably, but that they shouldn't forget where it all came from (Deuteronomy 8:10–16). "You may say to yourself, 'My power and the strength of my hands have produced this wealth for me.' But remember the LORD your God, for it is he who gives you the ability to produce wealth" (Deuteronomy 8:17–18). Sure, I work to earn money, but who gave me the job? Who gave me the strength and ability to do it? Our culture tells us there's a simple equation for success: "hard work + determination = success." We don't like to admit that there are more variables at play, far more than we could ever hope to control. When we look at the food on our table, we can remember that it's only there because God took care of those variables for us.

The necessary companion of gratitude is *contentment*. We're only happy with something when we feel like it's enough. Because we have it, we're good.

I work retail, and trust me, in America, contentment is not our thing. I've heard Thanksgiving referred to as "the day before Black Friday." Thanksgiving is about being content with what God has provided. Black Friday is not. Which day gets more attention?

We want more. In fact, we can hardly wait to throw away what we have so we can get the newest model. We want everything bigger, smaller, better, faster, with more cycles, better optimized, in this year's color, with bacon. Americans account for 5 percent of the world's population but consume enough to produce half of the world's solid waste. If God did only give us our *daily* bread—just what we needed for *that day*—we would *freak out*!

We are conditioned to look for more. To demonstrate this: think of the last time you wandered through a store wondering, "What might be nice to have?" Now, think about the last time you wandered through your house wondering, "What could I do without?" Perhaps we could take this prayer as a chance for re-evaluation. How much do we really need? Paul learned to be content whether he had a lot or a little (Philippians 4:12). With our warped perspective of our possessions, we have trouble being content with either.

The last and perhaps best way I can pray "Give us this day our daily bread" is to redefine "us." Remember, the first-person pronouns in the Lord's Prayer are all plural. This prayer can become a prayer of *solidarity*. Who is "us"? Include in "us" people who may not get their daily bread. Include the pastors imprisoned in Eritrea for their faith. Include communities of believers like my friends in Africa whose way of life is being decimated by a changing culture and climate. Include the Southeast Asian girls who are lost in the system of human trafficking. Include those in the corners of our own cities who struggle with food insecurity. They are all "us." Many people in this world are in danger of not getting their basic, physical needs met. We pray this prayer best when we stand and pray with them.

The Lord's Prayer can become a prayer of solidarity.

So there are several ways we can pray this prayer—seriously and sincerely. We just need the perspective of the one to whom we are praying—the giver of all good gifts. Our prayer can acknowledge our dependence on him, recognize and appreciate what he has given, and widen the circle of those on whose behalf we ask for bread.

THINK ABOUT IT

1. Have you ever faced a time when you knew the food you had was going to run out? What happened?

2. Have you ever done a purge of things you didn't need? How did that feel?

3. Have you ever had a concern that you thought was too small to bother God with?

4. What if God only gave you what you needed for today?

26

Forgive

"Forgive us our debts, as we also have forgiven our debtors. . . . For if you forgive other people when they sin against you, your heavenly Father will also forgive you. But if you do not forgive others their sins, your Father will not forgive your sins." (Matthew 6:12, 14–15)

I briefly served in pastoral ministry. I was not at a healthy church. About half the congregation participated in a "church health" survey, and after the consultant finished compiling the results, he told us, "I've never seen a church score this low." Dysfunctional churches don't usually volunteer to hear about how messed up they are.

There were good people there. Meeting Marvin, a 106-year-old member of the congregation, was one of the great blessings of my life. But there were issues. Among other things, some of the trustees were, perhaps, overly concerned with making sure their tithes were being spent acceptably.

Our second summer there, my wife-at-the-time was very pregnant. The parsonage where we lived was under-insulated and too big for its air conditioning unit. She was miserable, so I put in a request with the board to at least get a window unit for the bedroom.

At the next meeting, they declined that request and then agreed to put an awning over a church entrance that no one ever used. Amid mounting difficulties, that was my cue to move on.

While things like that stung, the real pain concerned my career. My original dream was to teach at a Bible college. People who graduate seminary and go into pastoral ministry get interviews. People who drop out of ministry to work at a home improvement store do not. That crash was hard, and I mostly put it on them.

Forgiveness was an issue.

The Lord's Prayer is short. That's the point (Matthew 6:7–8). If you're going to whittle things down and say no more than what absolutely needs to be said, this is it. The prayer has just four movements, and one is about forgiveness: "Forgive us our debts as we forgive our debtors" (Matthew 6:12). Forgiveness is the only theme that gets an extended discussion after the prayer: "For if you forgive others their trespasses, your heavenly Father will also forgive you, but if you do not forgive others their trespasses, neither will your Father forgive your trespasses" (Matthew 6:14–15). Forgiving others is essential (a point that gets its own parable in Matthew 18:21–35). If we're going to talk about the Kingdom, we have to talk about forgiveness.

Understanding forgiveness starts with understanding what's being forgiven. Verse 12 mentions "debts" and verses 14–15 say "trespasses," but Luke is clear that this is all under the umbrella concept of "sin" (Luke 11:4). To talk to our culture about sin in a way that doesn't sound like meaningless church gibberish (think the teacher in the Peanuts cartoons), let's start with how we experience sin. A person "sins" when they choose their immediate interests over someone else's well-being. The choice may look good right now, but the net result is that sin does damage.

If it does damage to us, our response is (in retrospect), "That was dumb." If it does damage to someone else, our response is, "That was wrong." We only start talking about "sin" when we realize that God has a stake in all this.

God takes sin personally.

When this sinks in, the blood drains from our faces. All the other effects of our sin pale in comparison (Psalm 51:4). We have violated something fundamental to the universe. Maybe the idea of a moral offense against a sovereign God doesn't really connect with our culture, but everyone can see that this world is broken. The Christian doctrine of sin is the awful realization that we are the ones who broke it. And we are still breaking it. Every time I choose my immediate interests over someone else's overall well-being, I break the world just a little bit more. And often the damage can't be undone.

All this damage has a compounding effect. We have all been hurt by someone else's choices. That hurt can take many forms—physical, financial, whatever. When I left my job at the church, I recovered from the financial impact in six months. The emotional healing took years. We often handle that emotional pain in ways that do more damage:

Someone causes me pain. *Vengeance* tries to stop the pain by giving the pain back to the offender. But it doesn't work. Even if we succeed in hurting them, our pain doesn't leave. In the end, two people are hurting. We didn't get rid of the pain; we multiplied it. *Resentment* passively hopes the offender will get hurt in return. This doesn't hurt the offender. Instead, every time we see them not hurt, the pain is compounded in us. In *bitterness*, the pain takes root and isn't really connected to the offender anymore. As a result, instead of paying the pain back, we pay it forward. We become toxic, spreading our pain to those around us. (That was me.)

This is what living in the "present evil age" is: hurting and being hurt. Pain compounding pain. To live in this world is to experience the pain of being harmed by other people's choices and to harm other people in turn.

In steps Jesus.

In the work of Christ, the old, broken age is giving way to the new, unbroken one. When damage can't be undone, the solution is that everything must be made new (Revelation 21:5). If our sin has broken the old age, the only way to get to the new age is forgiveness.

Forgiveness is the bridge between the old age and the new age.

This is true on a cosmic level. You may have seen a diagram that shows a chasm between people and God: sin is the chasm, and the cross bridges it. What is the cross? Forgiveness (Matthew 26:28).

Forgiveness is the bridge between the old age and the new age.

Forgiveness comes in two varieties—subjective and objective. Subjective forgiveness has to do with how I *feel* about the person who did the damage. Sin has consequences. While the consequences for the sinners themselves are not always obvious, they are real. Forgiveness means letting go of my desire to see the one who sinned face those consequences. I may want to see them *healed* (even if that's a rough process), but I no longer want to see them *hurt*.

What is God's subjective response to our sin? How does God feel about all this breaking we do? Apparently, he's pretty mad about it (see

Romans 1:18; Ephesians 2:3). This may be an uncomfortable truth. But I have no business telling anyone (much less God!) what he should or shouldn't feel or what boundaries to draw. I am grateful that God's fundamental characteristic is not anger, but love. In his love, he's done absolutely everything necessary to deal with his anger. That is what "propitiation" means (1 John 2:2; 4:10).

God's forgiveness is also objective. Subjective forgiveness doesn't want the offender to face the consequences. Objective forgiveness *removes the consequences*. It pays the debt. In fact, Jesus' word on the cross, translated "It is finished" (John 19:30), was often used exactly that way. It was written on a bill of sale to indicate "paid in full."

If God's forgiveness removes (in this life or the next) the consequences for all the breaking we do, how bad were those consequences? Look at the cross for the answer.

Pretty bad.

Jesus' death on the cross was the sum total of all the harm humanity has ever done to each other. In Jesus' death, all the brokenness caused by our sin died with him. When he rose, he brought something new.

We live in between the old and the new. The Kingdom is "now" but also "not yet." If forgiveness is the bridge between the two, and we live in between the two, this means we need to live in forgiveness. Forgiveness is the very atmosphere of the Kingdom of God. This has implications for how we live as citizens of the Kingdom.

First, *forgiveness must be reciprocal*. As Matthew 6:14–15 says, forgive and you will be forgiven. Don't, and you won't. But wait—do we forgive because God forgave us, or does God forgive us because we forgive others? Which comes first? Sometimes, like in the parable of the unforgiving servant (Matthew 18:23–34), God forgives first (cf. Ephesians 4:32; Colossians 3:13). Other times, it looks like we do (cf. Mark 11:25). Many versions translate Matthew 6:12 this way: "Forgive us our debts, as we also *have forgiven* our debtors" (NIV). It's like God will forgive us *in response* to our forgiving first. So which is it?

Neither.

The translation "as we *have forgiven*" makes too much of the Greek aorist tense. All the verbs in the Lord's Prayer are in the aorist tense, so I don't know why this one would be translated any differently. The aorist tense can indicate a past action, but it fundamentally has a more indefinite, almost timeless sense. God forgives. That's just what he does. We forgive. That's just what we do.

Forgiveness is the nature of the Kingdom. Forgiveness is the bridge between the broken world and the unbroken world. That's why unforgiveness is such a problem. Unforgiveness is unforgivable because it rejects the bridge itself.

It chooses our emotional pain over our healing. Our pain is part of the old world. We can't let it become part of our identity if we want to live in the new. Entering the Kingdom means being willing to release our emotional pain. God is not codependent. If we don't choose healing, he's not going to force us.

As with the rest of the Christian life, this isn't about perfection. It's about choosing to walk in the right direction. Jesus understands more than anyone how deep hurts can go. The great summary of the Lord's Supper begins with the oddly intimate and painful note: "On the night he was betrayed" (1 Corinthians 11:23).

God is patient as he leads us through the process of forgiveness. If we are to pray the Lord's Prayer every day, it also means we pray to "forgive our debtors" every day. Forgiveness is a process. Walk with Jesus in it. You don't need to feel 100 percent better on the first day. You just need to want your healing more than you want your pain.

The second implication of forgiveness in the "now but not yet" is that forgiveness is *ongoing*. People will keep sinning. We will keep being hurt. Forgiveness is not a rare exception; it's our lifestyle (Matthew 18:21–22).

Some hurts are so severe that they echo in our lives for years. I forgave that church for the thing about the air conditioner, but then I would hear about someone I knew from college getting a teaching position, and the pain and anger came right back. In her book *Forgiving What You Can't Forget*, Lysa TerKeurst suggests distinguishing the initial sin from its ongoing effects.[58] When you experience the ongoing effects, consider them new sins, new hurts that call for their own forgiveness. This doesn't mean you failed to forgive the first time. It means your brother has, in a sense, come back to you yet again (Luke 17:4).

Lastly, as we live in the "now but not yet," it would be great to bring healing not just to ourselves, but to others. Including those who hurt us. It's not an excuse, but the people who hurt us almost certainly did so because they had been hurt. (Grasping the hurt in my old church helped me forgive.) Many of the ways we deal with our pain just cause more hurt. Only forgiveness offers a chance at healing.

There are no guarantees. The people who hurt us may not think they need healing. They may not be interested in repentance. They may not want reconciliation. That's okay. Forgiveness is about what's going on in our hearts. Reconciliation would be great, but it is not required for forgiveness. In fact, the New Testament says that, without repentance, there are some people we need to keep at arm's length (2 Timothy 3:1–5). We can, however, still want them to experience healing, and we can still let go of the desire that they would be hurt. As a matter of fact, I saw the head trustee from my old church at my store just the other day. We smiled and said, "Hello." There have been no apologies, but I don't need any.

So why doesn't God's forgiveness work like this? Why does his forgiveness require repentance, while ours doesn't? Because God's forgiveness is objective. His forgiveness removes the actual consequences of our sin. But the consequence of our sin is alienation from God. Whatever brokenness we experience in the world is just a symptom of being alienated from him. For God, to forgive objectively is to remove that alienation.

The only solution for alienation is reconciliation. But reconciliation is necessarily a two-way street. Any relationship involves at least two people. A broken relationship only gets fixed if both want it fixed. If either one is not fully invested in fixing the relationship, it doesn't matter how much the other person works, sweats, bleeds, and cries to make the relationship work. One person alone can't heal a relationship. Not even God can do that.

God did everything he could for our relationship. Jesus wanted us to be reconciled to God enough to die for it. The rest is up to us. If we repent, we are forgiven and reconciled to God. As Jesus puts it, a right relationship with God *is* eternal life (John 17:3). It is deliverance out of a world that has fallen far short of the mark, and it is deliverance into a Kingdom where God's will is done and everything is as it should be.

Forgiveness is not tangential. It is not some "nice" thing to do. It is the heart of the gospel. If you want salvation—to "be made whole"—then enter into the "atmosphere of forgiveness" that is the Kingdom. Forgive and be forgiven.

That is how the Kingdom comes.

THINK ABOUT IT

1. What sins do we pretend don't do damage? What damage do they actually do?

2. Have you experienced God removing the consequences of your sin? What happened?

3. What has your experience of unforgiveness been like?

4. Whom do you need to forgive? Lysa TerKeurst would write the specific offense on a note card and pray, "I forgive this person for how their actions back then are still impacting me now. And whatever my feelings don't yet allow for, the blood of Jesus will surely cover."[59]

27

Deliver Us

"Lead us not into temptation, but deliver us from evil." (Matthew 6:13)

Nine years in, my marriage was not doing well. It would be another year before our marriage counselor told me that there were personality disorders in the mix. Without taking extreme measures, a long-term relationship was unsustainable. At the time, all I knew was that I was unhappy.

Once, my wife-at-the-time came to the store where I worked to get a few things. She found me at a department desk talking with an attractive coworker who had become a good friend. I talked with my wife, and as she walked away, I was embarrassed to realize that I would rather stay with my coworker than walk my own wife out. I was not in a good place.

That made the ill-conceived work Christmas party a total setup. I'm not much of a drinker, but my attractive, married coworker was a vodka and Red Bull kind of gal. I was already primed to make poor choices. It was not a good time to find out how I held my liquor.

The party was fun, but boundaries blurred over the course of the evening. Afterward, a few people decided to visit another bar. She invited me along. The only thing that saved me that night was a young man from the store with even fewer boundaries. His intentions with my friend became obvious as the night went along. By the time other coworkers intervened, insisting that he call it a night, it was so late that everyone just wanted to go home.

The next day, my coworker was uncharacteristically bashful. For her, the alcohol had clearly been in charge. I couldn't say the same. I didn't achieve some kind of victory that night. I was delivered.

That's where the Lord's Prayer ends: "Lead us not into temptation, but deliver us from evil" (Matthew 6:13).

An early Christian community couldn't handle that the last word in the Lord's Prayer is "evil," so they decided to come up with a nice little flourish they could say that would end the prayer on a positive note. "Maybe something about God's Kingdom and glory or something." Most likely, they wrote this in the margins of their church's copy of Matthew. Then, when someone went to make another copy, they saw the note in the margins and thought, "Oh, that has to be the real ending. I wonder how it ended up over there? Oh, well. I'll put it back where it goes." And we've been saying it ever since.

There's nothing wrong with, "For thine is the kingdom and the power and the glory forever, amen." It's just not how Jesus ended the prayer.

He ended it with evil.

We live in the "now but not yet." We still have to deal with the realities of living in a fallen world. If you think about it, that's what the entire Lord's Prayer is—our response to living in a fallen world. We pray for God's will to be done because we often see the opposite. That's why we still have daily needs to pray for. That's why we must keep forgiving and being forgiven: in this broken world, we keep sinning and people keep sinning against us. So, if we're going to be realistic about our situation, there is one reality about the old, fallen age that we can't ignore.

The devil.

That's right. Jesus doesn't just end the Lord's Prayer with "evil." He ends it with the phrase "*the* evil." In Greek, if you want to say, "the evil *one*" (as in, the devil), that's how you say it. Most times that Matthew uses the phrase "the evil," he's obviously talking about a person (Matthew 5:39; 13:49). Sometimes it's clear that this "person" is the specifically the devil (Matthew 13:19, 38). But in Matthew 6:13, almost every translation can only bear to put this in a footnote because who wants to end the Lord's Prayer with the devil? Well, if the devil is a reality of the old age that we can't ignore, where should we put him? Dead last works for me.

We still deal with the old age, and it would be madness to pretend that the devil isn't out to get us. When we woke up this morning, we woke up in a war zone. As we go about our day, we are often operating under heavy fire. We are being hunted. Ignoring this fact is a good way to get ourselves killed.

What's the devil's deal? The best way I've heard it put is based on Revelation 12:7–12. The devil wants to hurt God. But he can't. So, instead, he's doing everything he can to hurt the people God loves.

Since we have free will, the devil is mostly constrained to trying to get us to hurt ourselves. That's what temptation is. Technically, temptation is anything that increases the probability that sin will occur. But that's the English word. The Greek word, *peirasmos*, has a more varied sense of "seeing what you're made of"—a kind of "testing." It can be constructive, like refining metal in the fire. God does this (Hebrews 11:17). Or it can be destructive, hoping you fail the test. God doesn't do this (James 1:13).

When we ask God not to lead us into temptation, this is another way of saying, "Deliver us from the evil one." (Remember Hebrew parallelism.) It's what we get if we put 1 Corinthians 10:13 into prayer form: "God is faithful, and he will not let you be tempted beyond what you can bear. But when you are tempted, he will also provide a way out so that you can endure it."

But when the devil puts us in the fire to reveal our true colors, he's hoping they will be bad. He wanted to sift Peter like wheat (Luke 22:31) to show that he was nothing but chaff. The devil wants us to fail. So that's his strategy: increase the probability that sin will occur. If sin does occur, it causes damage. That's a win for him.

Including this in the Lord's Prayer provides a daily reminder that we will encounter forces that are trying to pull us away from God. It's an attempt to keep us on alert. Sin generally appeals to our unconscious mind, the part of our brain that is all about immediate rewards. Our unconscious mind isn't set up to process long-term costs. Therefore, operating on autopilot is an invitation to disaster, but staying aware helps. This prayer can prompt reflection. What temptations usually get us? What should we be on the lookout for?

Of course, Matthew 6:13 isn't advice. It's a prayer. This prayer is an expression of humility—a recognition that we could be undone. First, our alertness has limits. We can't maintain 100 percent vigilance all the time. Plus, things can come at us from left field. We weren't watching for them because we never would have thought of them. Or, as in the case of my work Christmas party, our inner resources could be so depleted that we're an easy target. In all these situations, we're going to need God's help to get out. This prayer is a great place to start.

So, yes, the Lord's Prayer ends with the devil. Until the Kingdom comes in its fullness, the pull of the old age is a daily reality. We could sum up Jesus' advice on prayer this way:

1. Take a posture of humility to God,
2. Remember that the small stuff matters,
3. Enter the Kingdom atmosphere of forgiveness, and, finally,
4. Keep turning our back on the world that is passing away.

Until the Kingdom comes, the old age is a daily reality.

Because it *is* passing away.

This is not the first time Matthew mentions the devil. In fact, the devil was in the chapter right before this sermon. When Jesus tells us to pray for deliverance, we are aware that he knows what he's talking about. In Matthew 4, we saw the devil tempt Jesus with everything he had. Jesus' temptation in the wilderness was the devil's head-to-head assault—his attempt to take down Jesus like he's taken down every other person in history.

But Jesus has come to herald a new age. He is beginning a new history.

So, for the first time, the devil lost.

The devil is a defeated foe. With Matthew 4 fresh in our minds when we read the Lord's Prayer, we remember that Jesus is already victorious in the battle to usher in the new age. We've already seen the powers of darkness melt in his presence. The victory Jesus had against his temptation in the wilderness is the victory he can have in our temptation, too.

Sun Tzu said that the ultimate skill is to defeat the enemy before they even get to the battlefield. This is what the devil has to do, because the second we stand and call on Jesus' name, he's done. No matter how strongly he attacks us, no matter how much we feel the pull of the old age, we have access to a power that is far greater. In Christ, the new age has been born in us.

The battle may rage on, but the war has already been won.

Deliverance is there for the asking.

The Kingdom is coming, and even hell can't stop it.

THINK ABOUT IT

1. Does the devil factor into your worldview much? Why or why not?

2. Why would anyone not want to pray this prayer?

3. Have you experienced deliverance from a temptation?

4. "Temptation" is anything that increases the probability that sin will occur, but that probability is never 100 percent. When is your resistance the weakest?

28

Treasure in Heaven

"Do not store up for yourselves treasures on earth, where moths and vermin destroy, and where thieves break in and steal. But store up for yourselves treasures in heaven, where moths and vermin do not destroy, and where thieves do not break in and steal. For where your treasure is, there your heart will be also." (Matthew 6:19–21)

Solzhenitsyn first experienced the thieves in one of the train cars that moved prisoners around the gulag "archipelago." There's no good English translation for the Russian word "thieves." Solzhenitsyn is not talking about individuals who steal things. He's talking about an entire subculture of thievery. This group thrived in gulag because they were organized, merciless, and had an endless stream of easy targets. In compartments designed for eleven people, thirty prisoners were crammed together, and the political prisoners were in no position to resist the thieves.

Solzhenitsyn describes a typical encounter: one of the thieves would descend from their good seats along the top,

> . . . most often a vicious boy whose impudence and rudeness are thrice despicable, and this little demon unties your bag and rifles your pockets—not tentatively, but treating them like his very own. From that moment, nothing that belongs to you is yours any longer. And all you yourself are is a rubber dummy around which superfluous things are wrapped which can easily be taken off.[60]

It wasn't just the thieves. Every step of the way, prisoners could be—and were—robbed of anything and everything. The rational conclusion was, "Keep as few things as possible, so that you don't have to fear for them."[61] Solzhenitsyn realized that this principle applied well beyond gulag. Over his ten-year ordeal, Solzhenitsyn felt he had discovered one of life's great secrets: "If you want, I'll spell it out for you right now. Do not pursue what is illusory—property and position: all that is gained at the expense of your nerves decade after decade, and is confiscated in one fell night."[62] Hard experience revealed to him that chasing after temporary things is a road to nowhere.

Solzhenitsyn agrees with Jesus: we need a serious audit of the things we value. "Do not store up for yourselves treasures on earth, where moths and vermin destroy, and where thieves break in and steal. But store up for yourselves treasures in heaven, where moths and vermin do not destroy, and where thieves do not break in and steal. For where your treasure is, there your heart will be also" (Matthew 6:19–21).

To English ears, "Where your treasure is, there your heart will be also" (Matthew 6:21) almost sounds redundant. We use the word "treasure" to mean something we care about (e.g., "Those kids are my treasure"). But talking about our "heart" also points to things we care about. So Jesus would be saying "The things you care about are the things you care about." That isn't very enlightening.

In Greek, however, there's a little more space between these terms. In the most basic sense, "treasure" is a place—a room or a box—where people put things to keep them safe. Then, secondarily, it is the things they put in that box. The act of putting them in the box would be called "treasuring" them.

Why do I put certain things in my box? Because I value them. They are important to me. They are where my "heart" is. Since my "heart" is the core of my being, whether I admit it or not, the things I put in my box are the things I build my life around. So what do I put in my box?

Another way to ask this question is: What am I investing in?

Jesus asks this question because what I invest in reveals my heart.

Let's make the question of "investing" more concrete: What do I spend my time, money, and energy on? This is not a rhetorical question. It is quantifiable. Of course, every person has their own unique answer, but Jesus says that all our investments are grouped into one of two baskets: things "on earth" or things "in heaven" (Matthew 6:19–20). My life is centered on one or the other.

So what does "storing up treasures on earth" look like? Matthew 6:19–21 stands at a pivot point in chapter 6. You can look either direction for an answer. In the first half of Matthew 6, the religious leaders invest energy in getting praise from other people. That is their treasure, and Jesus' point is that this has nothing to do with heaven. For the rest of Matthew 6, Jesus talks about the most obvious "earthly treasure"—material things.

Interestingly, then, Matthew 6 touches on almost the exact same things that Arthur C. Brooks, a social scientist at Harvard, concludes do not lead to happiness.[63] Based on hard data from extensive sociological research, Brooks confirms that money, pleasure (Matthew 6:22–34), power, and fame (Matthew 6:1–18) are all dead ends on the road to happiness (as Solomon shouts an "Amen!").

Jesus also points to the obvious fact that these things are ephemeral. "Do not lay up for yourselves treasures on earth, where moth and rust[64] destroy and where thieves break in and steal" (Matthew 6:19, ESV). Everything that belongs to the old age will crumble into dust. This is not a controversial statement, and it alone should rearrange all our calculations of where we assign value.

Jesus is supremely qualified to assert that there are, in fact, things that survive into eternity. We don't usually hear eternity brought up in discussions about strategic investing. Bringing eternity into our practical calculations radically alters the balance sheet, but Jesus challenges us that it would be ludicrous to leave it out. There are things that decay and pass away, and things that don't. The rational conclusion is that those things that survive into eternity are the only things worth investing in: "But lay up for yourselves treasures in heaven, where neither moth nor rust destroys and where thieves do not break in and steal" (Matthew 6:20, ESV).

Most people don't intentionally set out to build their lives around the pursuit of money, pleasure, power, or fame. Occasionally you'll hear of a billionaire who says something like, "Life is a game, and I'm winning!" Or maybe an Instagram influencer who says, "Life isn't worth living if there isn't a camera around." People like that strike us as a little . . . off.

However, Brooks points out that if we don't intentionally set out to build our lives on something else, money, pleasure, power, and fame are the pursuits that we all default to. They have automatic appeal and provide instant rewards, so we follow them like children follow the Pied Piper. If we're not intentional about where we invest our time, money, and energy, that's where they'll go. In other words, we are going to store up treasures on earth unless we deliberately decide not to.

> **We will store up treasures on earth unless we decide not to.**

Moreover, the things we invest in don't just reveal our hearts; they shape our hearts. The good news is that if we lay up treasures in heaven—if that is where we invest our time, money, and energy—we grow to care more about those things. Over time, they work their way to the center of our hearts.

What are these things of "heaven"? They are the things that survive into eternity. It's a pretty short list. The only things that survive into eternity are God and people (including you).

Only relationships are eternal. This starts with my relationship with myself. My own personal growth and self-care (real self-care, not just escapism) stores up treasure in heaven because I survive into eternity. Plus, this is the foundation for my ability to invest in anything else.

Then there's my relationship with God. More than anything else, this clearly lasts into eternity.

Lastly, I can store up treasures in heaven by investing in other people. This can mean both investing in relationships themselves and in trying to help other people. Both store up treasures in heaven because they mirror God's heart for people. Those relationships have merit, not as a means to something else, but because people are valuable in and of themselves.

To lay up treasure in heaven, then, is to intentionally build into my life opportunities to invest in myself, in God, and in others. In fact, it's not just building these into my life, but building my life around them. I need to make these opportunities regular and strategic, because successful investments are about small contributions made consistently over a long time. This doesn't just work for my savings account; it also works for my character. Plus, any choice to *not* pursue money, pleasure, power, and fame can simultaneously be an investment in heaven. As Jesus' one concrete example of "treasures in heaven" says, "Go, sell what you possess and give to the poor, and you will have treasure in heaven" (Matthew 19:21).

Interestingly, these "treasures in heaven" also echo Arthur Brooks's research. He concludes that four things lead to genuine happiness: faith, family, friends, and meaningful service to others.[65] We can sum this all up in one word: "love." To store up treasures in heaven, live out love. Jesus sums it up: "'Love the Lord your God with all your heart and with all your soul and with all your mind.' This is the first and greatest commandment. And the second is like it: 'Love your neighbor as yourself'" (Matthew 22:37–39).

It's hardly surprising that the "treasures in heaven" match, almost exactly, the things that make people whole and happy in this life. As people created in God's image who live in a world designed along the grain of his character, the Kingdom life is the life we were meant for. Even in this broken world, living a life that values the things God values is still the best bet.

Of course, living in a broken world means that bets don't always pan out. Sometimes sound investments still go bust. Don't worry. God is willing to wait years, even lifetimes, to see an investment mature. All we need to do is keep investing in what really matters.

If we don't see the returns here, that's okay. We weren't storing up treasures here, anyway.

THINK ABOUT IT

1. How do you see the "treasures on earth" portrayed in our culture? Give examples.

2. Why would the "treasures in heaven" be the "rewards" Jesus promises in Matthew 6:1–18?

3. Chart out how you spend your time and money. What does this say about what you value?

4. What eternal treasure could you invest in more?

29

The Eye Is the Lamp of the Body

"The eye is the lamp of the body. If your eyes are healthy, your whole body will be full of light. But if your eyes are unhealthy, your whole body will be full of darkness. If then the light within you is darkness, how great is that darkness!" (Matthew 6:22–23)

In a desolate area of South Africa, at the bottom of a cliff, is a small puddle that is one of the most dangerous places on earth. The "puddle" is actually the opening of a chute just big enough for a person to swim through. Twenty feet down, the chute opens up into Bushman's Cave—a submerged cave almost as tall as the Eiffel Tower and two and a half football fields wide. More people have walked on the moon than have walked on the bottom of Bushman's Cave. Three people have died there.

Don Shirley was involved in an attempt to recover the body of a diver from Bushman's Cave but barely made it out himself. Part of his breathing apparatus imploded, so he had to control his oxygen levels manually. After that, he got a helium bubble in his ear, which caused him to lose any sense of balance. Then came the vertigo. He only made it out because he was able to grab hold of the line leading to the surface.

Without that line, it would have been impossible to find the way out. A diver can't see the entrance. It's too small and no light from the sun makes it through. The walls of the cave are so far away that a flashlight doesn't help. "If you shine the light in any direction, it will disappear. The darkness will eat the light." As Don put it, the darkness is total.[66]

172

In Matthew 6:22–23, Jesus warns that the state of our soul is determined by the extent to which we allow the light in: "The eye is the lamp of the body. If your eyes are healthy, your whole body will be full of light. But if your eyes are unhealthy, your whole body will be full of darkness. If then the light within you is darkness, how great is that darkness!"

Our focus shapes how we see the world. The Pharisees, for example, were focused on getting praise from people (Matthew 6:1–18). This brought them status. And, in a shame and honor society, status could have considerable economic implications. The Pharisees loved that whole game. Because that's where their focus was, they were blind (Matthew 23:26). Their focus was so skewed that they couldn't see anything.

Could we have a better example of the power of focus than our current media echo chambers? Especially with social media, it is easy to construct an environment where we get one narrative and only that narrative. That narrative becomes our reality. But since we have different echo chambers, people standing right next to each other are living in different realities.

There are many things we can focus on, but for Jesus, the choice is binary: I am either focused on the light or on the darkness. Whatever I focus on is what fills my life. Either light comes in through my eyes or things go dark.

And, as Jesus says, that darkness is devastating. First of all, perception has a nasty way of becoming reality. It did for me when I interacted with customers at my store. I started viewing most people as needlessly grumpy and argumentative, so I had more unpleasant encounters with people than I needed to. If I treat people like they're grumpy, guess what? They get grumpy. It's a self-fulfilling prophecy.

I am either focused on the light or on the darkness.

Second, perception can be self-reinforcing. If our perspective is dark, then we're tuned to notice darkness more easily. We'll see it more, which will tune us to notice it even more. The darkness inside us feeds itself. Take chronic complainers, who even on the sunniest day can't do anything but look for clouds.

If an unhealthy eye is self-reinforcing, how can I make it healthy? How do I break out of that cycle to gain a healthier perspective?

There's actually not much I can directly choose. I can't directly choose my beliefs. They form more-or-less automatically based on the evidence at hand. I can't directly choose my feelings. They form more-or-less automatically based on my experience.

But I can choose where I point my eyeballs right now. I can choose to look at what's good in a situation more than what's bad. I can choose to give my attention to what's healthy and not what's unhealthy. In the moment, I can choose to focus on the light, not on the darkness.

I can make habits of these choices. Studies in neuroplasticity are showing that we can direct our attention in ways that will intentionally reorganize the way our brains work. Our immediate attention is the foundation for developing our overall focus. Our focus is the foundation for our life approach, and our life approach is the foundation for our well-being. Therefore, our attention is the most valuable resource we have.

That's Jesus' point: attention is foundational. Sure, our connection with God is what can transform our lives. But, just as the sun doesn't do any good to the divers in Bushman's Cave, our relationship with God has no impact if he never gets our attention. If God is the light, your attention is the eye that lets him in. Or not.

Here's the bad news: we live in the "attention economy." Businesses have learned how to monetize attention—our attention. This business model gives companies the incentive to harvest as much of our attention as possible. For instance, at one point, the CEO of Netflix said that their chief competitor was sleep. They can't harvest attention from people who are unconscious. So keep 'em awake and keep 'em watching.

Teams of people far smarter than you or I are studying psychology and neuroscience with the explicit goal of hacking our brains so that they can siphon away our most valuable resource: our attention. Everyone clamors for our attention. But they don't want to do anything with it. They don't want to inspire us to anything. They just want our attention to have it, to sell it. They want us numb.

The most basic way to do this is to turn our electronic devices into dopamine "slot machines." Dopamine is the "feel good" chemical in our brains. People who sit for hours at the "one-armed bandit" aren't there for a pile of nickels. They're there for the dopamine rush they get when the bells and whistles go off and the coins drop. They never know when it's coming, so they just keep trying.

This is how most video games work. Play long enough and we'll get that next achievement or win that next prize. This is why video streaming platforms automatically play the next recommendation. Maybe we'll like it as much as the last one. We just have to watch to find out. This is why our news feeds are literally endless. Keep scrolling long enough, and something interesting is bound to pop up. Our brains anticipate this reward, and it is physically painful to walk away from it.

The purpose of all this is to keep our attention, our most precious resource, on their platform. This can become an especially sad form of "storing up treasures on earth." It doesn't really store up anything; our focus is simply on chasing the next dopamine hit.

A slightly more sophisticated method for harvesting our attention is to trigger "activating emotions," emotions that make our "survival brain" think it needs to take over. It screams, "Stop everything! We need to pay attention to this, *right now!*" Generally, this involves getting us angry, scared, or horny as quickly as possible—preferably in the thumbnail picture or the first half of the headline. This is why "angry, scared, or horny" pretty much describes our culture right now.

This is not the freedom Christ died for.

What is the point of all this attention harvesting? What is it built on? The foundation for the entire architecture of our "attention economy" is that someone is hoping to sell you something.

Ad revenue. That's it.

It's all about material possessions—people trying to suck us into storing up treasures on earth. It's the pull to put Mammon on the throne of our culture and our lives. Jesus' saying that "the eye is the lamp of the body" is not necessarily about money. Luke quotes it without that context at all (Luke 11:34–36). But in our culture, at least, it circles back to exactly where Matthew put it.[67]

Instead of looking into this crazy kaleidoscope, we can choose to step back, see it for what it is, and regain some of our own agency. Our focus can shift enough to recognize that this whole system is the darkness reaching for us.

SERMON ON THE MOUNT

Turn it off and start looking to the light.

Be deliberate about what you give your attention to. Let the Spirit and Scripture reorient your focus. "Finally, brothers and sisters, whatever is true, whatever is noble, whatever is right, whatever is pure, whatever is lovely, whatever is admirable—if anything is excellent or praiseworthy—think about such things" (Philippians 4:8).

Where are your eyeballs pointing? No matter how much our culture tries to hijack your attention, it's still your choice.

THINK ABOUT IT

1. What has God done to get your attention in the past?

2. When does entertainment cross over into self-medication?

3. Why do you think monks traditionally emphasize silence and solitude?

4. Think of the devices you use the most and/or the media you consume the most. What's your reaction to the idea of giving it up for a week? (The stronger the reaction, the greater the sign that maybe you should scale it back.) For extra credit, search "dopamine fast" on YouTube.

30

Mammon

"No one can serve two masters. Either you will hate the one and love the other, or you will be devoted to the one and despise the other. You cannot serve both God and money." (Matthew 6:24)

No other nuclear reactor has had an accident like Chernobyl. Safety standards are very high at nuclear power plants because people understand the consequences of mishandling radioactive materials. But personnel at Chernobyl were not trained all that well, and the reactor design had issues.

On April 26, 1986, some safety systems were shut down to run a test. Water (being used as a coolant) hit the hot fuel, the fuel cracked, and excessive steam pressure caused cascading problems that led to two explosions. For the next ten days, radioactive materials sprayed all over the surrounding area until emergency workers had dumped enough sand, clay, and lead on the reactor to smother it. The direct health effects weren't as apocalyptic as we often think, but humanity got a reminder of what they were dealing with. One hundred thirty-four emergency workers got acute radiation syndrome—nausea, vomiting, fevers, and even some skin burns—which killed twenty-eight of them. In the surrounding area, 6,000 children got sick from drinking contaminated milk. They had an increased chance of thyroid cancer, which was fatal for fifteen of them.

Channeled correctly, radioactive materials can accomplish great things. Left unchecked, the effects can be nightmarish.

The New Testament seems to view money that way. Money can be great, but only if we keep it in its place. The problem is that it keeps trying to slip out of its place.

I like Dave Ramsey's program. I also get that the title "Financial Peace" is a lot catchier than "Financial Responsibility"—which is what the program is really about. By all means, we should handle our finances responsibly (1 Thessalonians 4:11–12). But many people aren't just trying to have peace about their finances. They are looking to their finances to bring them peace. That's not what finances were designed to do. But if we've given up on the Kingdom, if we don't want Jesus' program for rolling back the curse, what other options do we have? We'll just have to try to buy our way out of the brokenness of this world.

Judging by most of the political discourse in the United States, that's exactly what we're trying to do. Amazingly, in our ultra-polarized political atmosphere, we all seem to agree on this basic assumption: money is our hope for wiping away the old age and ushering in the new. The only question left is who would manage the money better. In this, our true national religion, should we have a hierarchical priesthood dispensing out the green paper sacrament, or should we have a priesthood of all citizens? How can Mammon best be served?

In Matthew 6:24, the term "Mammon" plays off the Hebrew word for that which is trustworthy, stable, and reliable. Luke makes it clear that Jesus is talking about money (Luke 16:1–13). Jesus personifies money as a rival deity to God. It's something else that we can turn to. Something different that we hope will deliver the paradise we want.

The New Testament repeatedly warns that money (in Greek it's usually "riches" or the word for "silver") is a terrible master. In the New Testament, money constantly shows up motivating unsavory behavior—religious leaders letting the temple turn into a marketplace (Matthew 21:12–13); Ananias and Sapphira lying about their donation (Acts 5:1–10); Greeks opposing the gospel because it hurts their bottom line (Acts 16:16–21; 19:23–29). Not to mention Judas. As much as we could speculate about why he betrayed Jesus, let's not forget—Judas didn't volunteer his service. Judas got paid (Matthew 26:14–16).

Money does things to people. It can foster arrogance (1 Timothy 6:17). It can choke the Word out entirely so it can't bear any fruit (Matthew 13:22). True, the Old Testament puts a lot of stress on God wanting to bless his people in tangible ways, but in the next breath, it pivots and says, "But then you'll get comfortable, and then you'll forget" (cf. Deuteronomy 8:11–20). There are different ways to interpret what Paul says in 1 Timothy 6:10, but the basic point is clear: Money is the root. Evil is the fruit (1 Timothy 6:9–10). You may say, "But that's just the *love* of money!" Jesus responds, "Good luck threading that needle" (cf. Matthew 19:23–24). The problem is not simply that money *can* become our master. The problem is that it *wants* to. There is a seductive quality to it. That's why Jesus says, "It is easier for a camel to go through the eye of a needle than for someone who is rich to enter the kingdom of God" (Matthew 19:24).

If money succeeds in becoming our master, it reaps death. Jesus talks about the "deceitfulness of riches" (Mark 4:19). Money doesn't deliver on its promises. The Greek word for "greed" is literally "have-more-ness" (cf. Luke 12:15). "Greed" is the feeling that my happiness depends on having more in general. "Coveting" is the feeling that my happiness depends on having something specific. I have the thing in my sights, and my inner voice says, "I would be happy if only I had that."

> **If money succeeds in becoming our master, it reaps death.**

But I wouldn't.

The "hedonic treadmill" is a staple in happiness studies. First, we want something. Getting it can be a thrill, but that doesn't last long. As for having it? We adapt to that. We get used to it and get bored with it. So we go looking for the next thing. Treadmill.

Finally, there's the obvious fact that money doesn't last. Either it goes, or we go, and money is powerless to stop that. "God said to him, 'You fool! This very night your life will be demanded from you. Then who will get what you have prepared for yourself?'" (Luke 12:20). James is even less subtle: "Now listen, you rich people, weep and wail because of the misery that is coming on you. Your wealth has rotted, and moths have eaten your clothes. Your gold and silver are corroded. Their corrosion will testify against you and eat your flesh like fire. You have hoarded wealth in the last days" (James 5:1–3).

Given money's limits, Jesus works hard to shake us free from that particular idol. After Jesus fed the five thousand, they tracked him down on the far side of the lake because he gave them bread (hardly a luxury item!).

He tells them, "You don't understand. I'm the bread. Forget that bread. It doesn't give you life. I do" (cf. John 6:26–35). Jesus puts riches in their place: "Man shall not live by bread alone, but on every word that comes from the mouth of God" (Matthew 4:4). "What good will it be for someone to gain the whole world, yet forfeit their soul?" (Matthew 16:26).

Once we reorient our perspective, money just isn't that big of a deal. For instance: Should the children of the Kingdom have to pay taxes? No. But who cares? Just pay it (Matthew 17:24–27; 22:15–21). If we serve the God who owns the cattle on a thousand hills (Psalm 50:10), stuff just isn't a problem (Matthew 14:15–21; 15:32–38; Luke 5:1–11). Don't worry about it. That's what the rest of Matthew 6 is all about.

So the heroes in the New Testament are people who either have nothing (like John the Baptist [Matthew 3:4] or Jesus himself [Matthew 8:20]) or who give up what they have to follow Jesus (like Peter and Andrew [Matthew 4:19–20] or Matthew [Matthew 9:9; see also Matthew 13:44–46]). As Jesus tells the rich young ruler, "Go, sell your possessions and give to the poor, and you will have treasure in heaven. Then come, follow me" (Matthew 19:21). Just to make it clear—this wasn't a personal issue for this particular guy. Jesus says the same thing in an open comment to anyone who wants to follow him: "Sell your possessions and give to the poor. Provide purses for yourselves that will not wear out, a treasure in heaven that will never fail" (Luke 12:33).

So, as a Christ-follower, what's the right posture to take toward money? Be deeply suspicious of it. View money (and possessions in general) like it's radioactive. If you handle it very carefully, you can do some good with it. But if you let your guard down and get sloppy, it *will* kill you.

One way to lessen the pull of Mammon is to make do with less. John the Baptist said that if you have two shirts, then you have one you can give away (Luke 3:11). The author of Hebrews urges us to be content (13:5; cf. 1 Timothy 6:5–6). A good way to foster contentment is to live below our means. I stumbled into this out of necessity, but I found it to be a great discipline for developing a healthy attitude toward money. Instead of asking, "How much can I spend?" I started asking, "How much can I *not* spend?"

During my first two weeks of graduate school, I was waiting for a friend to drive the bulk of my stuff to my new apartment. While I waited, the only dishes I had were a cup, a bowl, and a spoon. I survived just fine. Once my friend delivered the rest, it seemed kind of silly. I looked at all those boxes and thought, "Now I know that I don't need any of this." (Spoiler: you need a lot less than you think.)

This is the opposite of the "hedonic treadmill." As we start to appreciate all the things that money can't buy, a lot of the things it can buy start to seem pointless. Then, if we get a windfall or if our savings accumulate, the money isn't already spent in our heads. Instead, we can ask God, "Whoa. Wait. What am I supposed to do with all this?" Odds are, he has a few ideas.

Money, at the end of the day, is just a tool, a "little thing" (Luke 16:10). Nothing more. We can use it wisely or foolishly (Matthew 25:14–30; Luke 16:1–9). And if money is radioactive, giving fosters the attitude that keeps it from contaminating our hearts (cf. Ephesians 4:28). That is why every time rich people are mentioned positively in the New Testament, they are giving (cf. Matthew 27:57–60; Luke 7:4–5; 19:1–10; Acts 10:2; 16:14–15; 1 Timothy 6:17–19; Hebrews 7:1–2).

Money is meant to be a servant, not a master. Giving is how you "hate the one and love the other." It is how you put God on the throne and send Mammon packing. If you don't hold on to money, then money can't hold on to you. "It is more blessed to give than to receive" (Acts 20:35). Giving isn't losing; it's being set free.

1. In what ways is God a giver?

2. If we try to put a specific dollar amount to "How much is too much?" the answer is usually, "Just a little bit more than what I have." How can we focus on attitudes rather than amounts?

3. Are there things you're hanging on to that you could give away (and probably not notice that they were gone)? What things?

4. What is your favorite experience of giving?

31

Don't Worry

"Therefore I tell you, do not worry about your life, what you will eat or drink; or about your body, what you will wear. Is not life more than food, and the body more than clothes? Look at the birds of the air; they do not sow or reap or store away in barns, and yet your heavenly Father feeds them. Are you not much more valuable than they? Can any one of you by worrying add a single hour to your life? And why do you worry about clothes? See how the flowers of the field grow. They do not labor or spin. Yet I tell you that not even Solomon in all his splendor was dressed like one of these. If that is how God clothes the grass of the field, which is here today and tomorrow is thrown into the fire, will he not much more clothe you—you of little faith? So do not worry, saying, 'What shall we eat?' or 'What shall we drink?' or 'What shall we wear?' For the pagans run after all these things, and your heavenly Father knows that you need them. But seek first his kingdom and his righteousness, and all these things will be given to you as well. Therefore, do not worry about tomorrow, for tomorrow will worry about itself. Each day has enough trouble of its own. . . . "Ask and it will be given to you; seek and you will find; knock and the door will be opened to you. For everyone who asks receives; the one who seeks finds; and to the one who knocks, the door will be opened. Which of you, if your son asks for bread, will give him a stone? Or if he asks for a fish, will give him a snake? If you, then, though you are evil, know how to give good gifts to your children, how much more will your Father in heaven give good gifts to those who ask him!" (Matthew 6:25–34; 7:7–11)

Storing up treasures in heaven makes sense. Serving God and not Mammon is obviously the right choice. But you still need to eat. In fact, you have all kinds of practical, material needs. What about those? "So," you might ask Jesus, "if I put all my focus on pursuing the Kingdom, how can I make sure my basic needs get met?"

Jesus answers, "You can't do that anyway, so don't worry about it."

George Mueller was amazing at this. Over the course of his life in the mid-1800s, he ran five orphanages caring for over ten thousand orphans in Bristol, England. Although this was expensive work (the buildings alone cost over 100,000 pounds) he never made requests for financial support. Instead, he was a man of intense, persistent prayer. He prayed, he did God's work, and God routinely dropped what Mueller needed in his lap.

One of the most famous incidents was the morning the housemother of the orphanage let him know that there was nothing to feed the children for breakfast that day. He told her to take the kids to the dining room and have them sit at the tables as usual. Mueller came in, said a prayer thanking God for the food, and then everyone just sat there. The local baker knocked on the door. He couldn't sleep the night before. Sensing that Mueller would need bread, he spent the wee hours of the morning making three batches that he had brought to donate. Moments later, the milkman showed up because his cart broke down right in front of the orphanage. The milk would spoil by the time he got the cart fixed, so he gave it all to Mueller. It was just enough for all three hundred kids.

George Mueller may have been a legend at praying instead of worrying, but I'm not. I love it when a plan comes together. When it doesn't, I start to freak out just a little bit. I have a hard time not worrying.

Three times in Matthew 6:25–34 Jesus says, "Don't worry," and once he asks the rhetorical question, "Why worry?" If we're going to listen to Jesus here, we need to understand what worry is.

Worry is focusing on possible negative future scenarios that I do not control.

The Greek word for worry (*merimnao*) can have the much broader sense of "care," and this "care" can be a good thing (1 Corinthians 7:32–34; 12:25; Philippians 2:20). It can also just mean being preoccupied with something. Jesus corrects Martha for her "worry" simply because she was preoccupied with the wrong things (Luke 10:41–42). The "worry" in Matthew 6 is not this generic sense of "care." It clearly has a future orientation: What will we eat? What will we wear (Matthew 6:25, 31)? What about tomorrow (Matthew 6:34)?

Of course, most people don't worry that they might get invited to an ice-cream party. We worry about bad things. Like not having what we need. This is not some generalized "anxiety." Jesus' examples are specific—food, drink, clothes. Substitute whatever keeps you up at night. For me, it's whether my kids will find a way to make a living when they grow up.

Once we start looking into the future, we open Pandora's box. We don't know the future. We're just making this stuff up. We literally get worked up over imaginary things. And we can imagine all kinds of scenarios.

In *The Nature and Destiny of Man*, Reinhold Niebuhr observes that, like every other creature, people are contingent. They need things in order to stay alive. But unlike other creatures, people are consciously aware of this fact and able to project it into the future.[68] We don't just understand, "I'm hungry now." We understand, "I'm going to be hungry again tomorrow." This is why we "store up treasures on earth." We realize we may eventually need them. But our needs are theoretically infinite. There's always another "tomorrow."

If you're one of the day laborers Jesus is talking to, that day is literally tomorrow. But even if you're John D. Rockefeller, there is a "tomorrow" that you don't have enough for. So how much is enough? As Rockefeller said, "Just a little bit more." Our worry can outpace any amount of accumulation.

Whatever "nightmare scenario" we come up with, the problem is that we don't have control. This is the difference between worrying and problem solving. Problem solving focuses on things we have the power to influence. That's not worry. Worry isn't putting thought into what we can do; it's focusing on what we can't.

Having a job that helps pay the bills is not worry. Jesus says, "Don't worry," not, "Don't work." His illustrations about birds and flowers (that they don't do any work) picture God's care for us. Jesus isn't advocating irresponsibility. In fact, Paul insists on the exact opposite (2 Thessalonians 3:6–12). Jesus is telling us not to focus on contingencies we don't control. Whether I have a job or not, there's always another tomorrow to worry about.

Focusing on future contingencies we don't control paralyzes us. By definition, we can't do anything about them, but our worry won't let us look away. It may feel a bit like problem solving, but we're just chasing our tails. As Jesus points out, worry doesn't accomplish anything. It can't add a metaphorical cubit to our lives (Matthew 6:27; Luke 12:25–26). It doesn't change tomorrow (Matthew 6:34), but instead lets this imaginary tomorrow ruin our "today." We can't worry ourselves to life, but we can worry ourselves to death.

Worry doesn't accomplish anything.

So what do we do about worry? Jesus' answer is clear: trust God. Instead of being one of "little faith" (Matthew 6:30), remember the God we serve.

In Matthew 7:7–11, Jesus returns to this discussion about trusting God. He continues talking about physical needs (7:9–10), develops the idea of God as our loving Father (7:11), and keeps using the vocabulary of "seeking" (7:7–8). Whatever we're worried about, whatever we think we need, just ask. Hand it over to him. We can trust him to take care of us. "If you, then, though you are evil, know how to give good gifts to your children, how much more will your Father in heaven give good gifts to those who ask him!" (Matthew 7:11) That's the point of looking at the flowers and the birds (6:26, 28–29). God takes care of them.

The other aspect of trusting God is choosing to focus on the Kingdom (Matthew 6:33). The path Jesus lays out in the Sermon on the Mount is the progressive realization of the Kingdom. Commit to that path no matter what your worry tells you.

The thing about unhelpful inner chatter—whether it's fear, doubt, worry, or whatever—is that it won't just go away. But that doesn't mean it has to drive the car. Worry wants to take the driver's seat, but it won't take us anywhere (much less to the Kingdom!). Maybe we can't shut it up, but we can put it in the passenger seat and keep going anyway. We choose what we focus on. Focus on the Kingdom.

"But you could die!" says worry.

Spoiler alert! Everyone dies. Jesus even makes a nod to this when he talks about adding a cubit to our lives. At some point, our time is up. However that comes, would worrying about it have made any difference?

People die. Birds die (Matthew 10:29). Grass gets mowed down and burned (Matthew 6:30). Matthew 6 isn't a promise that God will never let anything bad happen. It's a promise that if we focus on the Kingdom and entrust the rest to God, he will do more than we ever could. "Not even Solomon in all his splendor was dressed like one of these" (Matthew 6:29).

He's the God who made manna fall out of the sky (Exodus 16). He's the God who got ravens to feed Elisha (1 Kings 17:1–6). He's the God who invented "endless bread sticks" (Matthew 14:13–21). And he said, "No one who has left home or brothers or sisters or fields for me and the gospel will fail to receive a hundred times as much in this present age: homes, brothers, sisters, mothers, children and fields—along with persecutions—and in the age to come eternal life" (Mark 10:29–30).

The deal is not that God takes care of our needs so we can go about our business. He takes care of our needs so we can go about his. If I seek the Kingdom first, will God really take care of my needs? Isn't the Kingdom worth trying to find out?

As the ship the *Dawn Treader* neared the end of its voyage, most of the sailors refused to go on. For Reepicheep the mouse, however, there was nothing that could stop him from continuing east toward Aslan's country. "My own plans are made. While I can, I sail east in the *Dawn Treader*. When she fails me, I paddle east in my coracle. When she sinks, I shall swim east with my four paws. And when I can swim no longer, if I have not reached Aslan's country or shot over the edge of the world in some vast cataract, I shall sink with my nose to the sunrise."[69]

The more we put the Kingdom first, the more "don't worry" takes care of itself. There's nothing "bad" to worry about because we are pursuing the only thing that matters.

THINK ABOUT IT

1. Have you experienced God providing in an amazing way? What happened?

2. How is seeking the Kingdom the antidote to worry?

3. How would your faith walk be different if you had an "abundance" mindset (that God gives and isn't going to run out) rather than a "scarcity" mindset?

4. What does "seeking the Kingdom" look like for you, right now? Is there a deeper way God is calling you to seek the Kingdom?

32

Judge Not

"Do not judge, or you too will be judged. For in the same way you judge others, you will be judged, and with the measure you use, it will be measured to you. Why do you look at the speck of sawdust in your brother's eye and pay no attention to the plank in your own eye? How can you say to your brother, 'Let me take the speck out of your eye,' when all the time there is a plank in your own eye? You hypocrite, first take the plank out of your own eye, and then you will see clearly to remove the speck from your brother's eye. Do not give dogs what is sacred, do not throw your pearls to pigs. If you do, they may trample them under their feet, and turn and tear you to pieces." (Matthew 7:1–6)

Even though I work inventory, I hang out in the cabinets and appliances department a lot. Kitchen design can take hours, so their computers have stools to sit on. Plus, most of my best friends work in CabApps.

When I first started thinking about writing something on the Sermon on the Mount, I was sitting at one computer, and the Wiccan Assistant Department Manager was standing at the other. I asked him, "Multiple choice: What is the most famous verse in the Sermon on the Mount. (A) 'Love your enemies, and pray for those who persecute you.'?"

"Ooh," he responded, having never heard that before, "That's good."

Well yeah, I thought, *Jesus is a major religious figure for a reason.*

Option (B) was the Golden Rule. He had heard that one. Option (C) was, "Judge not lest you be judged." His reaction to that one surprised me.

"That comes up all the time when I'm talking with Wiccans. 'Those Christians are so judgmental, and that's even in their own book!' But at some point, I'm like, 'You know, we're being pretty judgmental about this. How does that make us any better?'"

Matthew 7:1, "Don't judge, or you too will be judged," is a verse non-Christians love and Christians love to avoid. Often, we Christians begin a tap dance that focuses almost entirely on explaining what Jesus is *not* saying. It's true that he's not saying we shouldn't form any judgments. Later Jesus will talk about discerning (i.e., "judging") whether someone is a false prophet (Matthew 7:15–20). And so we use examples of the ways we should judge—what Jesus isn't saying—so we can go about our business of ignoring what he is saying.

That's what judgmentalism does.

Jesus spends an entire paragraph fleshing out what he means by judging. "Why do you look at the speck of sawdust in your brother's eye and pay no attention to the plank in your own eye? How can you say to your brother, 'Let me take the speck out of your eye,' when all the time there is a plank in your own eye? You hypocrite, first take the plank out of your own eye" (Matthew 7:3–5). *Judgmentalism is focusing on what's wrong with other people rather than looking at ourselves.*

Why do we do this? Now, when I say "we," I don't just mean Christians. My friend in CabApps recognized that this is a universal human tendency. As one radio DJ commented, the internet is proof that Christians don't have a corner on judgmentalism.

At its core, judgmentalism is a defensive move. But it doesn't defend us from something *out there.* It's a way to defend ourselves from our own feelings that we can't handle. Judgmentalism is a way to regain a sense of power when something threatens to make us feel "less than."[70] It says, "I'm not 'less than'! *You're* 'less than'!" This very act of judging empowers us. After all, a judge doesn't fear the defendant. They are not equals. The judge has all the power.

For example, I may want to avoid feeling impotent. Someone did something I feel is wrong, but I don't have the power to do anything about it. I get angry at their actions, and my anger has nowhere to go. The more enraged I become and the more impotent my rage is, the more I turn to judgmentalism.

More often, judgmentalism is sparked by a feeling of inner condemnation. Part of my subconscious mind is telling me that I am not good enough. If I haven't started dealing with my issues, this voice makes me feel powerless. I have no answer to it. To escape it, I turn it on someone else. *"They're not good enough!"*

This is a great way to avoid looking at things we don't want to see. We stuff our negative beliefs about ourselves away somewhere that is not consciously accessible. When we bury these beliefs, they become nasty little gremlins, wreaking havoc on our daily functioning. We can end up projecting our own faults (rightly or wrongly) onto others and railing against the exact things we struggle with (Romans 2:1, 21–24). The measure we use is the one used against us (Matthew 7:2). This is the hypocrisy so often trumpeted by the non-believing world, and that Jesus himself points out (7:5). As one porn star put it, the guys who protested her industry most vehemently on Sunday were the guys she danced for in the clubs the following Friday.

Where does this judgmental reaction take us? The first effect of judgmentalism is that judgment begets judgment (Matthew 7:1). As my friend in CabApps pointed out, little can trigger the judgmental response more than feeling judged. Being judged makes us feel "less than." What is our automatic response? Judge back.

This is where Matthew 7:6 comes in. On its face, it seems like a weird verse: "Do not give dogs what is sacred; do not throw your pearls to pigs. If you do, they may trample them under their feet, and turn and tear you to pieces." But if we look at the structure, it's fairly straightforward. There's a negative command ("don't give/throw") followed by a warning of bad stuff that will happen otherwise ("lest they tear you to pieces"). This is the same structure as Matthew 7:1: a negative imperative ("don't judge") followed by bad stuff that will happen otherwise ("or you will be judged"). These look like bookends to the discussion on judgmentalism. In fact, 7:6 is probably just a more colorful version of 7:1.

Jesus has already defined "judging" as pointing out what's wrong with everyone else (Matthew 7:3–4). Judging and giving unwanted advice— "Here, let me get the speck out of your eye"—are two ways of describing the same thing. People usually take the phrase "pearls before swine" to mean advice that falls on deaf ears. Think about it. What happened the last time you gave someone unwanted advice? How did that go? Does "lest they turn and tear you to pieces" sound about right? Jesus is echoing Proverbs: "Whoever corrects a mocker invites insults; whoever rebukes the wicked incurs abuse" (Proverbs 9:7).

When people feel judged, they judge right back. So we Christians have a problem: when many Christians hear this verse, they immediately feel judged. Because of the phrase's popularity in our culture, we don't hear Jesus saying it. We hear some hypothetical non-believer saying, "How dare you judge us!" And the dance begins. Instead of looking inward, we look outward. We get defensive and judge right back: "Yeah, Jesus says, 'Don't judge,' but we *need* to judge because *do you see what those people are doing?*"

In the Sermon on the Mount, Jesus doesn't care what those people are doing (1 Corinthians 5:12–13). He cares what's going on in our hearts.

Note that, in Matthew 7:6, we're giving holy things, pearls. This implies that our assessment of our brother (that speck in his eye) is right! There *is* something wrong with him. But 7:6 also points out how ridiculous it is to think that our righteous pronouncements will help. The people we're correcting are not in a place to receive. That should be obvious (hence "dogs" and "pigs"). If it's not obvious to us, it's because we are not seeing straight. Something is blocking our vision.

We are blinded by judgmentalism. We can't see them if we can't look at ourselves. This blindness is the second effect of judgmentalism. As Dallas Willard puts it, how does Jesus know that the judger has a plank in his eye? Because judgmentalism is the plank.[71]

Judgmentalism blinds us to others and to ourselves. In refusing to look at ourselves, we are blinded to our own faults. If we can't examine our own hearts, there's no hope of being freed from the sinful patterns hiding there. Maybe Jesus chose this as the last major topic in the Sermon on the Mount because this issue can prevent us from dealing with any of the others.

Judgmentalism blinds us to others and to ourselves.

Indeed, judgmentalism can lead to many of the attitudes the Sermon has warned us against. Because judgmentalism is, fundamentally, a failure of empathy. Judgmentalism consists of two emotions: condemnation ("you are less than") and self-righteousness ("I am better than").[72] Put those together, and empathy disappears. In fact, some people wallow in these attitudes long enough that they take a negative view toward humanity in general. But the problem with hating people is that you are one.

The only way out of judgmentalism is to rejoin the human race. Allow ourselves to be finite, flawed, and fallible. Only then can we extend that grace to others (Matthew 7:5). Only then can we recognize that there is no "them." There is only "us."

Working on my own judgmentalism, I found it incredibly powerful to emphasize our common humanity. When I saw people engaged in behavior that I viewed as a moral failure (which, in 2020, was pretty darn often), I learned to pray, "Forgive us our debts, as we forgive our debtors." The important thing here was to put the emphasis on "us." I identified myself with them. I recognized that I had plenty that needed to be forgiven too (cf. Luke 6:37–38). We were the same.

This requires humility, the antidote to judgmentalism.

Humility is key given the ambiguity in Matthew 7:1, "Judge not lest you be judged." "Be judged" is passive. Whom are we judged by? Jesus doesn't resolve this ambiguity. He embraces it. Yes, we are judged by other people when we judge. But there is also a greater judgment coming.

There is a Judge. And we aren't it.

Judgmentalism fades when we remember that one day we will all stand before God's judgment throne. There will be no "better than" or "worse than" there. Our pretenses will be stripped away. We will all be equal— broken humans in need of a Savior. None of us—not me, not the one I judged—will have any hope other than in the forgiveness that comes from the blood of Jesus Christ. On that day, there will be no judging and being judged. There will be no "us" vs. "them." There will only be, "There but by the grace of God, go I."

THINK ABOUT IT

1. What's your gut reaction when you hear, "Judge not, lest you be judged"?

2. Have you ever felt judged? How did you react?

3. What's your relationship with your inner critic? Is it the voice of a specific person who had a strong influence on you in the past?

4. How is our ability to extend grace capped by our ability to receive it?

33

Removing the Speck

"Then you will see clearly to remove the speck
from your brother's eye." (Matthew 7:5)
"What business is it of mine to judge those outside the church?
Are you not to judge those inside?" (1 Corinthians 5:12)

The first time I went to Starved Rock State Park, I had a hard time remembering that I was still in central Illinois. Just a few hundred yards from cornfields, the park has dramatic canyons and waterfalls cutting down to the Illinois river. I've been several times. I like heading out early while it's still quiet. I can sit at the bottom of one of the canyons and listen to the water. After about 10:00, families and groups from all over the world start flooding the trails.

The park has fourteen miles of trails. The farther they get from the visitor's center, the less clearly they're marked. People get lost a lot. I'm a map kind of guy, so I can usually help. I'll walk up to a group looking around in all directions, obviously unsure of themselves. Never once has someone taken offense when I tell them, "That trail takes you to Wildcat Canyon. The one you're on goes to a parking lot."

When people care about the destination, they don't mind a little course correction.

Offering course correction for life choices is trickier. It seems like it's none of our business and we have no right to tell people they're on the wrong path. It's not our place to judge.

When it comes to fellow believers, the New Testament seems ambiguous about this. On the one hand, it agrees with what Jesus says in Matthew 7:1–6: judging is a bad idea. James says, "Brothers and sisters, do not slander one another. . . . who are you to judge your neighbor?" (James 4:11–12). Paul uses his rhetorical questions to say the same thing: "You, then, why do you judge your brother and sister? Or why do you treat them with contempt? For we will all stand before God's judgment seat" (Romans 14:10).

While these two passages specifically say not to judge fellow believers, in 1 Corinthians 5:1–13, Paul says that he already has judged a problematic Corinthian believer (5:3), and then asks another rhetorical question: "What business is it of mine to judge those outside the church? Are you not to judge those inside?" (5:12). The implied answer is, "Yes."

So, wait—are we supposed to judge or not?

Look at it this way: our actions as believers can exist on a "disobedience" spectrum. On one end of the spectrum, we have obvious acts of disobedience. Say, a guy living in a sexual relationship with his stepmother (1 Corinthians 5:1). Gross. On the other end of the spectrum, we have actions that are not obviously disobedient (and may not be disobedient at all). Say, eating meat that may have been butchered in the process of worshiping an idol (Romans 14:2). On this end of the spectrum, things get fuzzy. The issue is whether the practice violates a standard God has for his people. Paul's discussion of these "matters of conscience" indicates that the farther someone is on the "not obviously disobedient" end of the spectrum, the more we need to leave that call between them and God. "Who are you to judge someone else's servant? To their own master, servants stand or fall. And they will stand, for the Lord is able to make them stand" (Romans 14:4).

On the starker end of the spectrum, we are dealing with things that clearly go against God's standard for his people. Part of following Jesus means accepting him as Lord. He's the boss. He makes the rules. When we commit to following him, we are agreeing to be held accountable to the standard God has for his people. And so, in matters of obvious disobedience, "Judge not lest you be judged" still works because we recognize that the measure we use is the same measure used against us. We all signed up for that. If I end up in such a bad place that I'm obviously not walking with Christ, I hope some of my brothers and sisters would intervene!

Why would I hope that? Why would we call out fellow believers on obvious acts of disobedience? In 1 Corinthians 5:1–13, this guy and his family have some serious issues going on. Left unchecked, those issues are going to bite them in nasty ways. They need an intervention; it's the loving thing to do. But Paul's main concern is that the intervention this guy needs is spiritual. Someone who accepts Christ but then lives in blatant disobedience is in a seriously dangerous spiritual place. It's like they got a "Jesus" inoculation—it's not strong enough to catch the real thing and produce a life-change, but it is strong enough to make them think they have so that they never really do. Paul's response is radical: "Hand this man over to Satan for the destruction of the flesh, so that his spirit may be saved on the day of the Lord" (5:5).

But there is a wider, communal concern here. As the community of God, what are we called to be? In ancient Israel, yeast was often used as a metaphor for sin. The metaphor emphasizes its ability to spread. It doesn't stay in one corner of the dough but defiles the whole thing. So the Passover feast (which celebrated Israel's redemption, deliverance, and freedom) was the beginning of the weeklong Feast of Unleavened Bread. Starting with Passover (their deliverance), all yeast was removed from the community. The point of the symbolism is that *they were freed to be pure.* The people of God are called to be holy. So Paul says, "Get rid of the old yeast, so that you may be a new unleavened batch—as you really are. For Christ, our Passover lamb, has been sacrificed. Therefore let us keep the festival, not with the old bread leavened with malice and wickedness, but with the unleavened bread of sincerity and truth" (1 Corinthians 5:7–8).

The call to Christ is a call to continuously grow in holiness, both individually and as a community. Sometimes, faithfulness to that call requires us to "judge those inside." This issue of course-correcting fellow believers falls under the subject of "church discipline." I'm mostly avoiding this language because "discipline" carries so many wrong connotations in our culture, but I mention it here to point out that the words "discipleship" and "discipline" are related. If you want the one, you cannot avoid the other.

The call to Christ is a call to continuously grow in holiness.

But we try.

When it comes to this call to greater holiness, we aren't doing it. Protestants may look down on the Catholic practice of confession because it could become mechanical, routine, lifeless. But we don't even ask our people to do that. We tend to just ask them to warm a pew for an hour or so every week while we make sure they know that Jesus loves them as they are, and maybe try to sell them on the features and benefits of Jesus. ("Hey, did you know that Jesus can help you manage your money?") Meanwhile, nearly every young, single adult in the audience is sexually active, and two-thirds of the men can probably remember the last porn they watched. And that's just one issue on Paul's list (1 Corinthians 5:11).

The "accountability" movement was a gesture in the right direction, but it seems to have fizzled. We had too much trouble figuring out how to focus on successes and not on failures. So what should this "prodding to greater holiness" look like? What's the format, the venue, the participants? How, exactly, should it work? The problem is thorny in the extreme.[73] But we can't find the answer if we're avoiding the question.

So why are we avoiding the question? Why are we reluctant to intervene with fellow believers engaged in obvious disobedience? First, perhaps we're afraid of their spiritual immaturity. As we've looked at in-depth, people do not naturally respond well to being corrected. We already saw in Proverbs 9:7, "Whoever corrects a mocker invites insults; whoever rebukes the wicked incurs abuse."

Yet Proverbs also holds out the possibility of the "wise person" who can respond well. "Do not rebuke mockers or they will hate you; rebuke the wise and they will love you. Instruct the wise and they will be wiser still; teach the righteous and they will add to their learning" (Proverbs 9:8–9). Christianity provides the exact resources (grace and forgiveness) to help us face our faults. Yes, we must gauge what an individual is ready to handle, but if they're never ready, something is seriously wrong.

Second, perhaps we're afraid of our spiritual immaturity. This is a perfectly rational fear. "Brothers and sisters, if someone is caught in a sin, you who live by the Spirit should restore that person gently. But watch yourselves, or you also may be tempted" (Galatians 6:1). Perhaps we'll be tempted by the same sin as that person, or by the lingering temptation of judgmentalism. If Jesus is always driving at attitudes, then attitude is key. Attitude is what makes the difference between harmful judgmentalism and a life-saving intervention. So Paul emphasizes restoring them gently. Also, many of these "intervention" passages imply or clearly state that it should be done in groups (Matthew 18:15–17). While this is based in the Jewish legal tradition (Deuteronomy 19:15), there's also some practical wisdom here. If other people also see a need for an intervention, then it's much less likely that I'm just venting my own neuroses.

Third, we're afraid of the mess. The "mess" simply is the lack of clarity. Does this situation merit an intervention or not? Is this any of my business? What is the morally right thing to do here? What is the effective thing to do here? Often, none of that is clear. We could get it wrong. Maybe we do the morally right thing in an ineffective way, and it just makes things worse. Or maybe *we* are morally out of line. We stand on the edge of this mess, this lack of clarity, the waters of chaos. Trying to walk across that water on our own is madness. Only the Holy Spirit can guide through this kind of thing. So Paul says, "You who live by the Spirit should restore that person" (Galatians 6:1). And when we fail, that's what grace is for.

Lastly, we're afraid of legalism. Are we just going to be piling up rules on people? This is spiritually toxic. Either they will (1) ignore the rules like a rebellious teenager ("It's too hard, so why even try?"), (2) think they are keeping the rules and thus become twice as much of a monster, or (3) settle somewhere in the middle, hoping they're "good enough" but living in constant (and correct) fear that they are not. Those responses are unacceptable, so instead we slide into what Bonhoeffer calls "cheap grace."[74] What do I have to do to be saved? Nothing, absolutely nothing. What do I have to do to be right with God? Nothing, absolutely nothing. What do I need to change? Nothing, absolutely nothing. What is Christ calling me to? Nothing, absolutely nothing.

When we ask, "What do I have to do to be right with God?" we get stuck on the dilemma between legalism and cheap grace, because the question itself betrays us. It shows that we are approaching God on transactional terms. We're relating to him like we're in a marketplace making a business deal. How much does this thing cost, and who is going to pay for it? The tendency of nearly every religion to devolve into a rules-based system shows a universal tendency to relate to God in transactional terms.

But that's not how God relates to us. He physically stepped into our shoes. He got a house in the neighborhood (John 1:14). He wanted his followers to understand that they were his friends and he loved them (John 15:9–15). Jesus didn't relate to us in transactional, market, business terms. He related to us in social, personal terms. Because the point of all of this is to know him. Personally. According to Jesus, that literally is eternal life (John 17:3).

So how do we know Jesus? Remember that the commands Jesus gives, all the imperatives in the Sermon on the Mount, are not arbitrary rules. They show us his heart. This is why obedience is the greatest way to know Jesus better. When we grow in holiness, we experience the heart of Jesus. We come to know him through having shared life experience. We have walked along the road with him. We have spent time in the trenches together.

So how can it be healthy to "judge those inside?" Only if we are the community of those who burn with a desire to know Jesus more.

THINK ABOUT IT

1. Which have you experienced more—legalism or cheap grace?

2. Have you ever had anyone correct you in a way that helped? How did they do it?

3. Are there people in your Christian community who would know if you were struggling?

4. How can you transition from a transactional relationship with Jesus to a personal relationship?

34

A Reckoning for the Church

"Why do you look at the speck of sawdust in your brother's eye and pay no attention to the plank in your own eye?" (Matthew 7:3)

Before we leave the discussion of judgmentalism, we need to talk. You may want to sit down for this, because judgmentalism is probably the great sin of the contemporary American church.

One of my friends had a horribly abusive husband. By the grace of God, she changed the place where she kept her gun. Otherwise he would have killed her. She had the strength to leave the relationship and become a single mom, but she lived in a small community. Eventually, the pastor of her church made a house call and asked, not the least bit subtly, when she was planning to leave town.

Another friend was raised in a strict religious home. It was an "every hair in place" kind of family. When he came out of the closet as gay, it was a disaster. To salvage the optics, they banished their own son to live with relatives thousands of miles away on the other side of the country.

A third friend tried several churches. She was a rail-thin white lady. The only racial unity she discovered was that she got a chilly reception no matter what church she took her black kids to.

My friends are just a few drops in the vast sea of "the judged."

There are two kinds of unbelievers in the United States—those who haven't heard of Jesus and those who have. The first group—those who haven't heard of Jesus—are pretty much all kids. Jesus is ubiquitous in our culture, so the only reason people haven't heard of him is because they haven't been around all that long.

Nowadays, church leaders are putting good thought into how to effectively reach kids. I'm not sure we've really wrestled with what it means to try and reach everyone else. Most churches *want* to reach grown-ups for Jesus. But most adult non-believers in our culture are not simply *non*-Christian. They are *post*-Christian. Personally. They've been there, done that, and got the church camp T-shirt. They encountered Christ on at least some level and said, "Thanks, but no thanks." We could speculate all day about why they made this decision, but if we ask them, most will cite judgmentalism.

In the last chapter, we looked at judging within the church. There are some behaviors we cannot condone in the life of fellow believers. When we draw a line—we have an intervention—they may not respond well. They may refuse to change, leave the church, and then cry, "Judgmentalism!" In that case, the charge of judgmentalism is a smokescreen.

But for every person who trumps up charges of judgmentalism, there are scores who have left the church because real judgmentalism scarred their lives. Listen to the average non-believer long enough and you will hear a story about how, in some way or another, it was communicated to them by people from the church (and often in the language of the church) that there was something unacceptable about them. They were judged. The Christian religion became profoundly invalidating. The very forms of Christianity (the language, symbolism, architecture, etc.) that we use to try to reach them for Christ were weaponized against them as instruments of emotional abuse. We can share our stories with them, and they may be interested, even affirming. But when we're done, they respond, "It's great that Jesus works for you, but he was used to beat me as a kid."

Untold horrors have occurred in homes in the name of Christ, but there have been plenty of corporate, public horrors as well. Many of us learned an evangelistic strategy that used "gotcha!" questions and sketchy logic to try to force people to admit that they were "sinners." "Have you ever told a lie? Then you're a LIAR! And liars go to HELL!" It was like someone read Matthew 7:1–6 and deliberately decided to violate it as much as humanly possible. "Let's dig for specks in their eye, judge profusely, then try to cram these pearls right under their feet!" Perhaps the idea was to announce forgiveness in Christ, but by the end, these poor random strangers weren't paying attention. They were too distracted thinking what jerks we were.

But it wasn't enough for us to ambush occasional strangers on street corners. No, we went nuclear with our judgmentalism. We declared war. Starting in the 1990s, these "culture wars" tried to use the full weight of our state and federal governments to force people to get the speck out of their eye.[75] Have protests! Sign petitions! Pass laws! Appoint judges! We waged this culture war with all the weapons of this world—political power and coercion. Many segments of American Christianity fight on, not realizing that we lost a long time ago. You'd think we would've seen that coming. Jesus told us: draw the sword, die by the sword (cf. Matthew 26:52). Which we did. But in losing this fight (in fighting at all), we lost far more than that. When we wage a culture war, we forget that wars do not make converts. They make casualties.

The field of our culture is strewn with casualties. Good luck getting any of them in your church building. For decades, one of my friends couldn't even enter a church without being triggered. These people are trauma victims. These are not people who casually walked away from the church. They are refugees who fled from the church for their very lives. If you think you can get them back with a catchy sermon series and a gift card to the coffee shop, you are not grasping the magnitude of the situation.

Christianity is a call to relationship—a relationship with the body of Christ and a relationship with God himself. The barrier between these post-Christians and the church is that there has been a breach in that relationship. The violation of their trust has reached the core of their being. They don't need evangelization; they need reconciliation. And reconciliation in a damaged relationship can only be found through repentance. The offending party must own the wrong they have done. There must be a deep and sincere apology, and there must be demonstration of an ongoing commitment to live a different way. A person who has come out of an abusive relationship would be irresponsible to re-engage the former abuser without this. We should understand better than anyone that there is no reconciliation without repentance. We just need to grasp the true nature of the reconciliation that needs to occur. If we want to have any hope of reaching these lost casualties of our culture, they aren't the ones who need to repent. We are.

Reconciliation in a damaged relationship can only be found through repentance.

1. What could this repentance look like?

2. Have you ever tried to witness to someone but it was not received well? What method did you use? Did they say why they objected?

3. Do you know anyone who has left the church? Have you asked them why?

4. Is there a non-believer you could ask about their experience of Christianity? (Note: Try to get beyond their *opinion* of Christianity to their *experience* of it. Also, try to say as little as possible unless they ask.)

35

Do Unto Others

"So in everything, do to others what you would have them do to you, for this sums up the Law and the Prophets." (Matthew 7:12)

M Scott Peck tells the legend of a dying monastery.[76] After centuries of persecution and secularism, all that was left were five monks, all over seventy, who lived in the decaying mother house. Sensing the end, the abbot decided to visit a rabbi who sometimes stayed in a hovel in the forest nearby. Perhaps the old man would have some wise advice.

The rabbi was happy to see the abbot but had no consolation for him. "It is the same in my town," he said, "Almost no one comes to the synagogue anymore." So they spent time crying together, reading Torah, and talking about deep things. As the abbot was finally leaving, the rabbi said, "I have no advice to give. The only thing I can tell you is that the Messiah is one of you."

This was a cryptic message. The abbot shared it with the other monks, and they wondered, "Does he mean that one of us five is the Messiah?" As the days went by, they thought about who it might be, if it were true. "Obviously not Thomas. He's crotchety. And yet, out of nowhere he often speaks a truth we need to hear. He might be the Messiah." One by one, they started overlooking each other's rough edges and realizing that each person had a unique contribution to make. As Peck puts it, "As they contemplated in this manner, the old monks began to treat each other with extraordinary respect on the off chance that one among them might be the Messiah. And on the off, off chance that each monk might be the Messiah, they began to treat themselves with extraordinary respect."

People from the surrounding towns often came to picnic on the monastery grounds. These visitors started to sense that something was different. Feeling the deep respect among the brothers, some of the visitors were drawn to spend time in the monastery talking with them and praying. Eventually, one young man asked if he could join their order. Then another. Then another. Within a few years, the monastery became a thriving order again.

After I first heard this story, I tried to bring this attitude back to the store where I worked. I confess I didn't maintain it for long, but while I did, something shifted. With every person I encountered—the bossy lady who didn't know her kitchen's measurements, the inarticulate contractor who reeked of weed, the grumpy coworker—I asked myself, "What if they have the unique contribution that the world desperately needs?" Rather than treating them as "difficult people," I started treating them with respect. Indeed, I treated them the way I wanted to be treated.

Matthew 7:12 is the second bookend of the Sermon on the Mount, echoing Jesus' opening discussion of "the Law and the Prophets" (Matthew 5:17–20). Jesus has given us his definitive description of life in the Kingdom. Matthew 7:12 is his concluding summary: "Do to others what you would have them do to you" (Matthew 7:12). If we had to distill the Sermon on the Mount into one dominant thought, this is it.

So what is this dominant thought? What is the core of the Christian ethic? When preachers and teachers try to sum up basic Christian morality, they often talk about integrity. Integrity is fine, but our Western individualism betrays us here. Integrity has no necessary relationship to other people. It is a quality you simply have in yourself. You can sit alone in your living room and have all kinds of integrity.

That's not the Kingdom. Jesus is surprisingly unconcerned with this kind of individual, personal morality. For Jesus, "living out your faith" is about how you treat others. Christian morality is about respect. Do you treat everyone you meet with dignity, as a fully human being? Thus, the paragraph on judgmentalism (Matthew 7:1–6) led us to the core attitude of empathy. In Matthew 7:12, Jesus summarizes his sermon by stating that the Kingdom is not just about feeling empathy. It's about living out empathy: "So in

For Jesus, "living out your faith" is about how you treat others.

everything, do to others what you would have them do to you, for this sums up the Law and the Prophets."

How does someone expound on the Golden Rule? It's a summary sentence. It's *the* summary sentence. It's a rephrasing of what James calls "the royal law" (James 2:8): "Love your neighbor as yourself." The entire Sermon on the Mount is Jesus expounding on the Golden Rule. In fact, Jesus says that the entire Law of Moses and the writings of the prophets elaborate on this one principle. They're all just applications.

We still need them—the applications put meat on the idea so it's not this abstract thing floating out there. Do you want your brother to treat you with contempt? No? Then don't treat him with contempt. The same goes for objectification, sincerity, judgmentalism, etc.

But we need the summary principle, too. Otherwise, we might miss that the applications do not exhaust the principle. There is no comprehensive list of rules to check off. That was the Pharisees' trap. Jesus has been combating it this entire sermon.

In fact, the attitude of legal nitpicking often makes its way into the discussion of the Golden Rule itself. (Calling it the Golden *Rule* doesn't really help!) Some folks make a big deal of the fact that other sages (Socrates, Confucius, etc.) state it negatively: "What is hateful to yourself, do to no other" (Hillel).[77] It's as though these teachers are simply saying what behavior we should avoid. Jesus, however, states this rule positively, as though he's saying what behavior we should actively pursue. This sounds nice, but the distinction is artificial. This is Jesus' summary of his sermon, and the instructions in the sermon are, more often than not, stated negatively, "Don't do this." Perhaps we could paraphrase the Golden Rule in a way that avoids the issue entirely: "Treat others the way you want to be treated."

In a word, our actions should be guided by empathy. We might think that we wouldn't need the reminder. A healthy human brain is hard-wired for empathy. But acting on that empathy can get complicated.

For instance, if I'm going to treat people the way I want to be treated, how do I want to be treated? Ideally, I want to be treated in a way that genuinely promotes my overall well-being. But sometimes I don't. I either let others devalue me or I devalue myself. I settle for that which does not promote my overall well-being. How I want to be treated grows out of what I believe I'm worth. Do I love myself? Do I grasp that I am created in the image of God and loved by him? Do I therefore have affection for myself that inspires a willingness to be stretched for my own benefit? Only when I value myself rightly will it be a good thing for me to treat others the way I want to be treated.

We are all created with the same value, but a further complication is that we are also all created unique. To treat others the way I want to be treated, I need to act in their best interests. But since we're all unique, it takes time and effort to understand what their interests are. It's easy to project ourselves onto others—to assume that they would think and feel about their situation the same way we would. But they don't. So the first act of treating people the way we want to be treated is to listen. That's the only way to understand their context. Empathy asks, "How would I feel, not in my shoes, but in their shoes?" Only once we answer this can we get some idea of how we would want to be treated.

But, more than that, our empathy often gets short-circuited. Sometimes we don't recognize that others have as much value as we have. Sometimes we don't want to recognize this. Sometimes I want to do what I want to do, and I don't want to be bothered by how it affects anyone else. This is pure selfishness.

We want our freedom, but, as social beings, we also want to live in community. John Stuart Mill, a favorite philosopher of the American founding fathers, was huge on individual freedoms. But he also realized that some of our choices affect the people around us. To keep a society functioning, he advocated the "harm principle": one person's freedoms end when they cause (or could likely cause) physical harm to someone else.

This may be a good principle for governing society, but for a Christ-follower, the "harm principle" is an entry-level application of the Golden Rule. For Christians, the overriding concern is not "my freedom" but "your value." Paul said, "Though I am free and belong to no one, I have made myself a slave to everyone, to win as many as possible" (1 Corinthians 9:19).

At the very least, the Golden Rule drives a nail through selfishness by insisting that we recognize the value of every person we affect, especially people in whom that value might not be immediately obvious—people who don't look, believe, or live like us. Love is meant to be universal

(Matthew 5:46–48). It even includes people who have acted like jerks to us. We don't judge (Matthew 7:1). We have mercy (Matthew 5:7). We forgive (Matthew 6:12, 14–15).

This doesn't mean living without boundaries. Quite the opposite. If someone is pushing one of my boundaries, I can reverse the roles and ask, "If I were pushing this boundary, would I expect them to accept that behavior?" If the answer is no, then enforcing my boundary is treating them the way I want to be treated.

Life can get foggy. When it does, return to the Golden Rule. It is a beacon that can guide us through this mess in a way that reflects God's heart.

We can think of the various areas of our lives as spokes of a wagon wheel radiating from a central hub. Of course, that hub needs to be Jesus. He is the organizing center for our lives. But what does this mean in everyday life? Jesus has lots of advice and instruction for how I relate to all the people I encounter in the different settings of life. But the heart of Jesus that radiates into all the spokes, filling them, defining them, turning them into an integrated, functioning whole is, "Do to others what you would have them do to you."

THINK ABOUT IT

1. Pick any ethical teaching in the Bible. How does it illustrate the Golden Rule?

2. How does God himself display the Golden Rule?

3. Where do you see the tension between freedom and community in our culture?

4. What's a situation where you could give up a freedom in order to communicate value to someone else?

36

The Narrow Path

"Enter through the narrow gate. For wide is the gate and broad is the road that leads to destruction, and many enter through it. But small is the gate and narrow the road that leads to life, and only a few find it." (Matthew 7:13–14)

The community college in my town has a great program where high school juniors and seniors can take classes for dual credit. My daughter asked her honors Algebra II teacher for a recommendation letter to the program. This was weird because she was failing his class. With the end of the second quarter looming, her grade was hovering stubbornly in the high 50s. Algebra II is hard. My daughter says she's seen most of the "smart kids" cry in that class. Since it was "honors" Algebra, I floated the idea of stepping down to regular Algebra for the second half of the year.

My daughter chose to stay. She decided to stick with honors Algebra, not in spite of the fact that it was hard, but because it was hard. It was pushing her in ways she had never been pushed before, and she saw this as an opportunity to grow as a person. She impressed the pudding out of me (and got the recommendation letter from her teacher).

Not many people deliberately choose the hard path.

Someone once asked Jesus, "Are only a few people going to be saved?" (Luke 13:23). In his answer, echoed in Matthew, Jesus clearly says, "Yes." "Enter through the narrow gate. For wide is the gate and broad is the road that leads to destruction, and many enter through it. But small is the gate and narrow the road that leads to life, and only a few find it" (Matthew 7:13–14).

Jesus has just summarized the entire Sermon on the Mount by reminding us that every single human being has the same value we do (7:12). Now he tells us that most people are on the road to destruction? How could anyone possibly be okay with this?

Actually, no one should be. Much of the Sermon on the Mount walks in the "wisdom literature" tradition. The point of this tradition is to honestly look at the way things are. I picture a grizzled older guy saying, "Look, kid. This is just how it is, like it or not." Jesus isn't saying it's good that the wide path leads to destruction or that he likes the fact that many (most?) people end up going that way. It's just the way things are. We can whine about it, but that won't change it.

Why is the path to destruction wide and the path to life narrow? A possible clue is that many "enter" by the wide gate, but few "find" the narrow gate. "Finding" the narrow gate involves intentionally looking for it, whereas "entering" the wide gate is more automatic. Do most people live their lives intentionally, or are they mainly on autopilot? Ask anyone whose profession is aimed at helping people achieve greater wholeness—counselors, personal trainers, life coaches: Do most people reflect on where they are and actively develop themselves into fuller people, or do they plod through their crappy jobs, get drive-through on the way home, and watch Netflix until they pass out?

It's painfully true that most people slide their way into destructive patterns of living. Whether we're talking about spiritual growth or a more secular "personal development," few choose to strive to grow as people. How common is it to deliberately pursue growth? In the context of the Sermon on the Mount, how common is it to actively work to become the kind of person Jesus describes?

Not that common.

The very word "work" is triggering in some Protestant circles. "Work? WORK? We're saved by grace, not by works!" The whole debate is a red herring. At best, the debate sucks up oxygen we could use trying to walk the life path Jesus lays out for us. At worst, we may conclude that it's wrong to try—that Christianity isn't active, it's passive.

Which is clearly ridiculous. Of course Christianity is active. Life is active. Jesus doesn't tell us to sit in the right chair. He tells us to walk the right path.

The path we are called to "enter" is the Kingdom (Matthew 5:20). It is life (Mark 9:43). It is the righteousness that is Jesus himself (Matthew 5:10–11). It is the path Jesus lays out in the Sermon on the Mount. In these three chapters, Jesus has been like a person marking a path through the forest, putting reflective markers on trees so we can know if we're going in the right direction.

Even if the path is clearly marked, walking it still takes work. The word "narrow" that Jesus uses (Matthew 7:14) implies difficulty and discomfort. Walking this path involves continual seeking. "Okay, I should forgive. But how?" "I should treat everyone with respect. But how?" "I should trust God for my needs. But how?"

The good news is that we do not ask these questions in a vacuum. Who shows us how? Jesus. Who gives us the power to do what he shows us? Jesus. Who sustains us when the path is hard? Jesus. Even after all the work, when we seek and then find, our response is, "Thank you, Jesus."

Who gives us the power to do what he shows us? Jesus.

Just live with the paradox: we work our tails off and yet experience the entire thing as grace. This is exactly what the guy who wrote "It is by grace you have been saved" did: "But by the grace of God I am what I am, and his grace towards me was not in vain. On the contrary, I worked harder than any of them, though it was not I, but the grace of God that is with me" (1 Corinthians 15:10). Paul's earlier analogy for the Christian life could not have been more active:

> Do you not know that in a race all the runners run, but only one gets the prize? Run in such a way as to get the prize. Everyone who competes in the games goes into strict training. They do it to get a crown that will not last, but we do it to get a crown that will last forever. Therefore I do not run like someone running aimlessly; I do not fight like a boxer beating the air. No, I strike a blow to my body and make it my slave so that after I have preached to others, I myself will not be disqualified for the prize. (1 Corinthians 9:24–27)

Paul doesn't say to walk the path Jesus laid out; he says to run it.

We may not like the idea that most people don't find this path. Neither does Jesus. That's why he's saying this. He's shouting to anyone who will listen that the path is here. It's available. It can be found.

Are you on it?

THINK ABOUT IT

1. Why do you think people often don't see the destruction at the end of the path they're on?

2. What's a good habit you've had a hard time building? Why?

3. Why are you reading this book? What do you hope comes of it?

4. What could help you pursue Jesus' path?

37

False Prophets

"Watch out for false prophets. They come to you in sheep's clothing, but inwardly they are ferocious wolves. By their fruit you will recognize them. Do people pick grapes from thornbushes, or figs from thistles? Likewise, every good tree bears good fruit, but a bad tree bears bad fruit. A good tree cannot bear bad fruit, and a bad tree cannot bear good fruit. Every tree that does not bear good fruit is cut down and thrown into the fire. Thus, by their fruit you will recognize them." (Matthew 7:15–20)

Thomas Keating tells a story about a Sufi master and his students. One day, the Sufi master was outside on his hands and knees sifting through the grass looking for the key to his house. Some of his disciples came along and asked if they could help. So there they were, all on their hands and knees, wandering around his yard looking for his key. Eventually, one of them asked, "Master, do you have any idea where you might have lost your key?" The master replied, "Of course. I lost it in the house."[78]

If happiness is getting in the house, the point is that there are plenty of people who will help us look for happiness in places we will never find it. One thing that makes walking the narrow path difficult (Matthew 7:13–14) is that the wide path has a lot of hype men.

As we saw in the last chapter, the wide path is easy because it's more or less automatic. Traveling on it is like stepping onto a conveyor belt. I just go with my gut, and my gut takes me along for the ride. This means that I'll never step onto the narrow path unless I get challenged in some way. Someone needs to point out that the wide path is taking me somewhere I don't want to go, and that something needs to change.

A false prophet won't do this. At the end of the Sermon on the Mount, Jesus warns, "Watch out for false prophets. They come to you in sheep's clothing, but inwardly they are ferocious wolves" (Matthew 7:15). A true prophet—one called by God—tells people what they need to hear; a false prophet tells them what they want to hear. "They dress the wound of my people as though it were not serious. 'Peace, peace,' they say, when there is no peace" (Jeremiah 6:14).

Whether our false prophets today claim to be speaking for God or not, they fit this pattern. Like any decent con artist, they are great at reading people. By wrapping their scheme in something people already want to believe, the message sells itself. Con artists aren't magicians. They succeed because people lie to themselves. "For the time will come when people will not put up with sound doctrine. Instead, to suit their own desires, they will gather around them a great number of teachers to say what their itching ears want to hear" (2 Timothy 4:3). This is called "confirmation bias." We're less critical of things that fit what we already believe (or want to believe).

We are also naturally inclined to trust people who are "like us." So false prophets figure out how to camouflage themselves. They find all the visible "boundary markers" we set up to distinguish who is "in" and who is "out." They learn to look like "us," act like "us," and talk like "us." This is their "sheep's clothing" (Matthew 7:15). Some get so good at demonstrating these "boundary markers" that they do it better than we do. Then they become leaders. Think of the Pharisees. What they're saying sure sounds right. They can quote Torah better than anyone.

False prophets figure out how to camouflage themselves.

But their character doesn't resemble the Kingdom of God at all. "By their fruit you will recognize them" (Matthew 7:16). We don't have to wonder what this "fruit" is. It's the fruit Jesus has been talking about this entire sermon—character that mirrors the heart of God. Do these people show the character of God in their own lives? Does their message foster that character in others? That's the fruit we're looking for.

I saw a news clip in which a child asked a political leader how to know what authorities he could trust. It's a powerful, profound, and timely question. This paragraph is Jesus' answer. When it comes to the "authorities" we look to, do they display or produce the kind of character Jesus describes in the Sermon on the Mount? Do they treat all people—men and women—with respect? Do they speak sincerely? Do they live from a heart of grace? Do they love universally? Are they unconcerned about status symbols? Do they hold money and possessions lightly? Are they empathetic? These things show a heart that has good roots (Matthew 7:17–18). Show me a person like that, and I want to hear what they have to say.

What about those who do the opposite? They regularly call people names and objectify women. They use words as tools to manipulate others. They seek revenge for the smallest slights, and their love has clear limits. They're all about the show and all about the Benjamins. Their natural reflex is to point the finger at everyone else. Such people will not hesitate to use us up and spit us out, just like the teachers of the law who "devour widow's houses" (Mark 12:40; cf. 2 Peter 2:3). Moreover, they have a date with a furnace (Matthew 7:19). Hitching our wagon to that train is not a winning strategy—for this life or the next.

Still, Jesus is not looking for perfection. He's not out to cancel someone for a single failure. In Matthew 7:17–18, "fruit" is plural, but in 7:19, it's singular. The tree that is cut down and burned isn't producing *any* good fruit. No one gets to be 100 percent on point. But what's the typical fruit I see from the person I'm listening to? What fruit does listening to them tend to produce in my own life?

If I'm serious about what path I want to be on, I need to surround myself with people who are calling me to that path. In my news, my entertainment, my friends, my leaders, I need to be intentional about whom I let speak into my life. Their fruit will become my fruit.

THINK ABOUT IT

1. We tend to retreat into echo chambers to escape the barrage of different viewpoints that are out there. What's the danger in this?

2. Have you ever seen good content that was wrapped up in a bad attitude? What results did it produce?

3. Think of the attitudes in the Sermon on the Mount (respect, sincerity, grace, love, inner devotion, generosity, trust, empathy). How do the voices in your life (particularly the media you choose) measure up to this list?

4. As the saying goes, "You are the sum of the five people closest to you." How can you surround yourself with people you aspire to be?

38

Lord, Lord

"Not everyone who says to me, 'Lord, Lord,' will enter the kingdom of heaven, but only the one who does the will of my Father who is in heaven. Many will say to me on that day, 'Lord, Lord, did we not prophesy in your name and in your name drive out demons and in your name perform many miracles?' Then I will tell them plainly, 'I never knew you. Away from me, you evildoers.'" (Matthew 7:21–23)

Jesus is not interested in the results that usually interest us.

The feeding of the five thousand is one of the most famous stories in the Bible. Crowds had been following Jesus around Galilee for days, but only one kid thought to pack a lunch. Jesus used the boy's fish and chips to feed the entire crowd (with plenty to spare), and we usually end the story there. But John keeps going (John 6:1–70).

Jesus and the disciples crossed the lake during the night. In the morning, the crowds saw that they were gone and went running around the lake to catch up to them. Clearly, Jesus had built up a fan base. But Jesus isn't interested in numbers. He's interested in hearts. So he gives a sermon so challenging—that they should seek him, and him alone—that he loses all of them. He began the day with at least five thousand "followers." He ended it with twelve.

Jesus measures success differently than we do. This is important for us to know because he's the judge.

For most of the Sermon on the Mount, Jesus has danced in the fuzzy intersection between the "now" and the "not yet," between the old age that is passing away and the new age that is breaking in. It often seems like what he says could apply to either this life or the next life. Here at the end of the sermon, that ambiguity vanishes. When Matthew says, "that day" (Matthew 7:22), it is prophetic shorthand for "the Day of the Lord." This is Judgment Day.

> Not everyone who says to me, "Lord, Lord," will enter the kingdom of heaven, but only the one who does the will of my Father who is in heaven. Many will say to me on that day, "Lord, Lord, did we not prophesy in your name and in your name drive out demons and in your name perform miracles?" Then I will tell them plainly, "I never knew you. Away from me, you evildoers!" (Matthew 7:21–23)

This paragraph makes almost everyone nervous. First, we're fond of making the distinction between "nominal" Christians and truly committed Christians, but that's not the distinction Jesus makes. Jesus distinguishes between those who talk about him a lot ("Lord, Lord") and those who actually do what he says.

The scary thing is that when Jesus talks about the wide and narrow paths (Matthew 7:13–14), he's talking to an entirely Jewish audience. He is not standing with the religious "in crowd," thumbing his nose at the vast sea of heathen scum. No, he's talking to folks who should be "in" and warning them! He's telling them to pay attention to what path they're on. Being part of the "in" group is not the same as being on the right path. Evidently, the "many" who say to Jesus, "Lord, Lord" (Matthew 7:22) are also the "many" who are on the wrong path.

It gets worse. When I was in Bible college, my fellow students and I couldn't help but notice that the folks Jesus said he didn't know were people who were *doing ministry*! Spectacular ministry! They were driving out demons and working miracles. If these people weren't close to God, who was?

Prophesying, casting out demons, working miracles—there is no more impressive ministry a person could hope to do. And on the day of judgment, it doesn't mean anything. Judgment Day is not a job performance review. Jesus is not going to look at your metrics to see if you met or exceeded your stretch goal.

He's going to look for a life that shows a transformed heart.

The "will of my Father"—the obedience that Jesus is looking for—is exactly what he's been talking about this entire sermon. It is the "righteousness" that surpasses the Pharisees. It is the visible transformation of character that causes the world to glorify God. It is our heart renewed to express the heart of God.

It's not about being good enough. It's about living from a heart surrendered to him. Did his work in our lives bear at least some fruit? Were we walking on the right path?

For this question, the specific tasks we did along the way are meaningless.

This is where it got personal for me. I wrote a lot of this book on my clipboard in the home improvement store where I work. When my coworkers and I were kids, none of us said, "I want to work retail when I grow up!" It took me years to accept that this job really was part of who I am. Even then, I still hated it. I swam in anger, depression, and bitterness for eight years until I finally started to see ways in which my job was a blessing.

First, I never confuse my job with my identity in Christ. There is no temptation to think that my meaning and value is found in the tasks I do at work. Many of my ministry friends are not so lucky. When you're standing in front of people talking about God all the time, those lines can get really blurry. But ministry is just a different set of tasks you perform. On Judgment Day, Jesus is going to look past all of that.

It took me thirteen years to recognize the second blessing. I looked around and realized that since retail is a challenging environment of short, often emotionally charged encounters with total strangers, it is a near-perfect laboratory for learning how to love people. I'm not saying that I've mastered it. My workplace is a good laboratory precisely because it can be so hard. I just figured out that it's what I'm supposed to be doing!

Here's what I'm discovering: learning to love people is simply learning to see them the way God does—seeing them through his love for them. When I see people the way God does, I experience something of God's heart. This means that in learning to love people, I get to know God better. Retail has become a vehicle for knowing God more.

God took me out of vocational ministry and put me in retail to draw me closer to him.

God is speaking. It doesn't matter if you're a peasant working in the fields, a stay-at-home parent, a missionary in the jungle, or the CEO of a Fortune 500 company. These are not ends; they are means. Meeting Christ there doesn't mean asking, "How can my relationship with God make me more effective at this task?" It means asking, "How is God using this task to draw me closer to him?" That's the end everything is working toward. Preaching to ten thousand people in a multisite megachurch is great for the congregation. But they're not with you on Judgment Day. How has God's heart been formed in you?

> **How is God using this task to draw me closer to him?**

This breaks down all the compartments we split our lives into—work, home, church, play, whatever. These don't just flow out of our relationship with God; they pour into it. When it comes to our hearts, they have no meaning in and of themselves. They only have meaning for us as we meet God there.

Theology 101: God is everywhere. Start looking for him there. If we focus on meeting Jesus in all our experiences, then we spend our entire lives getting to know him. Then there is no fear in the final judgment (1 John 2:28). When we stand before him on that day, he'll remember all the times we walked with him in the mundane and the glorious, in the dedicated work and the laid-back downtime. As old friends, he'll be bursting at the seams waiting to see us—waiting to cry out, "I know you!"

THINK ABOUT IT

1. Social scientists often measure religious involvement by (1) who checks the "Christian" box and (2) how often they attend church. Why is Jesus looking for something else?

2. What form of ministry seems most impressive to you or is most praised in your community? Why?

3. Can you think of a time when people thought your life demonstrated the difference Jesus was making in your heart?

4. What area of your life seems unrelated to God? How could you seek him in it?

39

Building Your House

"Therefore everyone who hears these words of mine and puts them into practice is like a wise man who built his house on the rock. The rain came down, the streams rose, and the winds blew and beat against that house; yet it did not fall, because it had its foundation on the rock. But everyone who hears these words of mine and does not put them into practice is like a foolish man who built his house on sand. The rain came down, the streams rose, and the winds blew and beat against that house, and it fell with a great crash." (Matthew 7:24–27)

I work in a home improvement store. I see people building houses, and I see people making life choices. People who make unwise choices often end up paying for them. One contractor was famous for overcharging while under-performing. Once, he used a forklift to remove a lady's entire roof. But that's not the worst part. It rained that night.

On another job, an elderly lady hired him to renovate her bathroom. As the job went on, he realized that she would keep paying whatever he said he needed to finish the next phase of the project. Eventually, instead of giving him another $10,000, her son shot him to death. In construction, as in life, you reap what you sow (Proverbs 22:8).

Building codes may seem complicated, tedious, and expensive, but they exist for a reason. Ignore them, and someone is going to get electrocuted, the toilet won't drain right, or the basement will flood. A friend of mine in plumbing had a guy who wanted to put a wood-burning stove in his garage. These require expensive, double-walled stainless-steel pipe. He just wanted to use the existing duct work. "You can't," my friend said, "It's too hot. It'll melt the pipe and burn your garage down." His response: "I don't care."

In the Sermon on the Mount, Jesus has laid out the "best practices" for life construction. Now it's up to us to decide if they're worth the effort. Often, they strike us as unrealistic—pie-in-the-sky stuff. The truth is we are the ones who are unrealistic. We use gas lines for water, then rage when the fittings leak.

We would love to build a Thomas Kinkade house that basks forever in the sunshine under a rainbow. But that's not the world we live in. At the end of Matthew 7, Jesus steps back into that "wisdom literature" way of talking. He even uses the words "wise" and "foolish." There will be thunderstorms, floods, and hurricanes. That's life. Jesus tells us how to build a house that will stand up to that.

One reason we may avoid Jesus' way is because it seems to cost too much. This is the paradox of the Kingdom—it costs everything and it costs nothing. It all depends on the value we place in these shadowlands. This sermon is dangerous only to those who cling to shadow values. It proclaims that a house built on them is doomed. Our only options are to surrender those values—trade them for Kingdom values—or have them stripped away. We cannot cling to smoke and fog.

Instead, we can build a house on Kingdom values. The secret is that this house is more durable in both this life and the next. In this broken world, we ground ourselves in things that will last. Therefore, the house we build can endure anything this life can throw at us.

So where do you need to start your "life renovation"? What needs to die? What "treasure" do you need to let go of? What little "kingdom" of yours do you need to let fall?

Now, building a house takes time. Reorienting the way we live—the way we relate to God, to others, to ourselves, to the world around us—takes practice. So even if we decide we do want to build our life on the foundation Jesus has laid in the Sermon on the Mount, we won't be experts overnight. We need to take this stuff into the arena and get bloodied up a bit. As the saying goes, "Anything worth doing is worth doing badly until you learn to do it well!"

As we build, we need to offer ourselves grace. As Christians, we tend to be surprisingly unforgiving of our own failures. But failure means we tried, and that alone is a win. When we fail, we can prayerfully reflect on what happened, preferably with other Christians, and see what we might try next. That's how we grow. We only ultimately fail when we don't learn from our failures.

As I was writing these chapters, there were times I failed miserably to do what Jesus was saying. A voice in my head would say, "That's the exact opposite of what you just wrote. If this stuff can't be lived out, it's meaningless gibberish." (Guess whose voice that was.) But another voice answered, "The power of the Sermon on the Mount is not negated by the times you failed; it is revealed through the times you succeeded."

Give yourself permission to grow—however messy that process is.

Start small. Jesus covers just about every area of life in this sermon. If I go through the sermon, list all the areas where I'm falling short, and try to work on all of them at once, I'll be overwhelmed. That's not how the Holy Spirit works.

Chances are, there is one area that he is calling you to grow in right now. Which one? The one that sticks in your mind because you don't want to deal

> **Give yourself permission to grow—however messy that process is.**

with it. But because the Holy Spirit is committed to forming Christ in you, he won't let it go. You can pray about it, submit it to him. Start looking for resources to help with the "how" questions and trust the Spirit to lead you to them.

Of all the areas where this sermon challenged me, judgmentalism was the worst. Once I recognized my judgmentalism, overcoming it seemed impossible. I couldn't even conceive of a mindset without it. It took a full year (including working with a professional life coach) for Jesus to break me free of that one. But he did. What area of this sermon seems impossible to you? Take it to him. I can think of few prayers more likely than this to qualify for the promise, "I will do whatever you ask in my name, so that the Father may be glorified in the Son" (John 14:13). Also, don't be afraid to hear from unconventional sources. You may have noticed that a lot of the people I cite in this book aren't Christians. This shouldn't be a surprise. Paul was a missionary who traveled an entirely un-Christianized world. He often found people who already had a strong moral compass (Romans 2:12–15). They were good people who were waiting to meet Jesus. When they did, he was not completely unfamiliar to them.

Yes, plenty of people pursue the lie, but there are also many who seek the truth. If Jesus is the truth, then any truth they discover is truth about him. If what they've learned helps me on my path to know Jesus more, I'll use it! If the fruit's good, let's put it in our pack and take it on the journey!

If any non-Christians have read through this entire book, I'm honored. But I sense that Jesus' challenge is aimed mostly at those who thought they had already gotten off the fence. That was me in my "wading in the shallows" moment. I had the horrifying realization that I had spent my entire life in the church but had made almost no progress in some of the areas Jesus emphasizes. I had read Jesus' words a ton. I just hadn't done them.

If you close the cover of this book and walk away saying, "Good study. Very interesting. What's next?" you missed it (cf. James 1:22–25). Reading a book about building a house doesn't mean you built a house. In the Sermon on the Mount, Jesus is calling to you to start building. How will you respond?

"To the Jews who had believed him, Jesus said, 'If you hold to my teaching, you are really my disciples. Then you will know the truth, and the truth will set you free'" (John 8:31–32).

We all live in the shadowlands. In this sermon, Jesus shows us the way out. He invites us to leave behind this dying world and join him in the life of the Kingdom.

Jesus is calling.

The Kingdom is near.

THINK ABOUT IT

1. Before this study, were there any teachings of Jesus that seemed impractical? Have your views changed?

2. Did you try to implement any of Jesus' teachings over the course of reading this book? How did it go?

3. Begin with the end in mind: What do you want people to say about your character at your funeral?

4. What particular issue from this sermon is the Holy Spirit speaking to you about? What ideas do you have for how to work on it? What issue do you need to take to him in prayer?

40

Appendix: The Beatitudes for Small Groups

A friend of mine said that the Beatitudes are like an onion—you keep peeling back new layers, and each one kind of makes you cry. They are not the sort of thing you dig into, exhaust, and then move on. They deserve to be sat with, meditated on. So here are some ideas for how they can prompt further discussion after you're done with this book, perhaps in a small group setting.

For any given beatitude, ask:

1. If a person fit into this category, what virtues would they have?

The Beatitudes aren't commands—"be this." Some aren't even inherently good. But there are virtues that they point to or grow out of. For example, we mourn simply because living in a fallen world means suffering loss. That's not great. But mourning does imply some level of *authenticity*. If we are crying out to God, it may even imply some level of dependence on him.

2. How is this beatitude countercultural or counterintuitive?

The Beatitudes are shocking. Some go against popular culture (say, *pure of heart* or *meek*). Some seem to go against *religious culture* (hence the long history of trying to spiritualize the *poor of spirit* and those who *mourn*). Some just seem to go against reason (how can you be happy about *mourning* or being *persecuted*?). There's paradox here, and the purpose of paradox is to crack open the shell of our worldview so we can see something new.

3. How is this characteristic linked to its reward in *this* life?

The middle six rewards are all in the future tense: "For they will . . ." But when? There is ambiguity in the Kingdom. To some extent it is "now." To some extent it is "not yet." Jesus doesn't resolve this tension. So how do we see each beatitude play out in *this* life? It may do so (1) because the Kingdom has started breaking in; and (2) because this world was created by God in the first place. Although it is broken, the world often still operates along the grain of his character.

4. What examples of this do you see in Scripture?

This is another way of exploring the previous question. We often don't know how to recognize these Beatitudes playing out in our daily lives. But we expect to see them in the Bible, so that may be an easier place to start.

5. How does this beatitude find ultimate fulfillment in the *next* life?

When Judgment Day comes and the Kingdom is established once-for-all, there will be no more ambiguity. What kind of hope does it provide you to know that, on that day, those who mourn will be comforted? The merciful will receive mercy? The pure in heart will see God?

6. How have you seen or experienced this in your own life?

Jesus is clear that all these things he's saying only matter when the rubber meets the road. In answering this question, we glorify God for the ways he has worked in our lives, and we encourage each other to keep walking on the path he marked out.

7. How do you see this in Jesus?

If the Beatitudes are a portrait of a citizen of the Kingdom, how much more are they a portrait of its King? One reason Jesus became a human being was so that he could show us how human beings are actually supposed to live. This is why we talk about "following" him. He is the model we are called to imitate.

Looking at Jesus' life and ministry, we will find examples of these Beatitudes at work. We don't have to follow this line of questioning for long before we find ourselves at the foot of the cross.

At the cross . . .

Was Jesus poor in spirit? If someone is so stressed that he literally sweats blood, he's overwhelmed and desperate.

Did Jesus mourn? Crying out, "Why have you forsaken me?" sure sounds like grieving a loss. Even if Jesus is simply quoting David in Psalm 22:1, he's quoting it because he is taking every curse on himself. He is bearing the full brokenness of the world. He is, on the cross, experiencing every grief everyone (including David) ever felt.

Was Jesus meek? A guy hanging on a cross isn't forcing anyone to do anything. And yet, "I, when I am lifted up from the earth, will draw all people to myself" (John 12:32).

Did Jesus hunger and thirst after righteousness? If righteousness, in this context, means living out the Kingdom life, then yes. Jesus was fulfilling his unique role in the kingdom. Moreover, this role he fulfilled on the cross is what opens up the possibility of righteousness to all of us. In the end, Jesus desired righteousness enough to die for it.

Was Jesus merciful? In the extreme. He didn't just extend mercy in the abstract to everyone far away. He extended mercy to the people immediately responsible for putting him on the cross. Refusing to "other" them, he cried out, "Father, forgive them, for they do not know what they are doing" (Luke 23:34).

Did Jesus have a clean heart? Absolutely. That's the only reason his sacrifice was accepted (Leviticus 1:3).

Was Jesus making peace? "For God was pleased . . . through him to reconcile to himself all things, whether things on earth or things in heaven, by making peace through his blood, shed on the cross" (Colossians 1:19–20).

Was Jesus persecuted? The cross was the ultimate act of the world rejecting him. "Though the world was made through him, the world did not recognize him. He came to that which was his own, but his own did not receive him" (John 1:10–11).

We are citizens of the Kingdom. If the Beatitudes are a portrait of our King, then the final version of that portrait shows him hanging on a cross. Brush stroke by brush stroke, it shows us who our Master is, and who we are called to be. Some strokes are beautiful, some are melancholy. In the end, they all say, "Whoever wants to be my disciple must deny themselves and take up their cross and follow me" (Matthew 16:24). It is the ultimate reversal that the way of blessing is the way to the cross. But for those with eyes to see, the picture of the Beatitudes is a portrait of the way of life.

The way of blessing is the way to the cross.

Notes

1. C. S. Lewis, *The Chronicles of Narnia* (New York: HarperCollins, 2010), 767.

2. A lot of the content of these chapters is separated out and sprayed all over the Gospel of Luke. In fact, many phrases and themes show up later in Matthew itself. Did Matthew compile a bunch of disconnected "Jesus sayings," or did Jesus, like a good preacher, reuse solid material in different contexts? There's no reason to choose. However, Matthew presents this sermon as a cohesive unit, so we're going to treat it as such.

3. In fact, in Matthew 23:8–10, Jesus says that the Messiah is *the* Teacher.

4. Fine. John doesn't specifically say that Jesus walked through the door. He does make sure to point out that the door was locked, though. So the point still stands—the physical state of the room should have prevented Jesus from entering, but it did not.

5. Tony Campolo, *Who Switched the Price Tags?* (Nashville: Thomas Nelson, 2008).

6. A. J. Harbinger and Johnny Dzubak, "4 Disciplines that Lead to Happiness and Meaning: Arthur C. Brooks," Feb. 14, 2022, in *The Art of Charm,* produced by The Art of Charm, podcast, podcasts.apple.com/us/podcast/4-disciplines-that-lead-to-happiness-and-meaning/id212382281?i=1000551008717.

7. M. Scott Peck, *The Different Drum: Community Making and Peace* (New York: Simon and Schuster, 1987).

8. Alvin Plantinga, *God, Freedom, and Evil* (Grand Rapids: Eerdmans, 1977).

9. Stephen Covey, *The 7 Habits of Highly Effective People* (New York: Simon and Schuster, 1989), 203–234.

10. Dale Carnegie, *How to Win Friends and Influence People* (New York: Simon and Schuster, 1981).

11. Ellis Amdur and John Hutchings, *The Thin Blue Lifeline* (Edgework, 2011), 6.

12. N. T. Wright, *Justification* (Downers Grove: InterVarsity, 2009), 89.

13. Jon Ronson, "When Online Shaming Goes Too Far," TED, ted.com/talks/jon_ronson_when_online_shaming_goes_too_far/transcript?language=en.

14. Andrew Marantz, *Anti-Social* (New York: Viking, 2019), 262–270.

15. Peck, *The Different Drum*, 86–90.

16. Rory Miller, *Conflict Communication: A New Paradigm in Conscious Communication* (Wolfeboro, NH: YMAA, 2015), 19.

17. Elizabeth Elliot, *Through Gates of Splendor* (New York: Harper & Row, 1957), 172.

18. "Persecution is God's Word Fulfilled," *The Voice of the Martyrs*, March 2021, 4.

19. "Eritrea: Senior Year Lockdown," *The Voice of the Martyrs*, September 2020, 4.

20. Andrew Brunson, *God's Hostage* (Grand Rapids: Baker, 2019), 166.

21. Todd Nettleton, "Middle East: The Moment He Accepted Christ," Sept. 26, 2020, in *VOM Radio*, produced by The Voice of the Martyrs, podcast, vomradio.net/episodes/detail/middle-east-the-moment-he-accepted-christ.

22. Meredith Foster, "Page 62: Brant Hansen," Sept. 25, 2020, in *The Unfolding*, produced by New Life Media, podcast, podcasts.apple.com/us/podcast/page-62-brant-hansen/id1460841077?i=1000492464559.

23. Robert Farley, "How Many Died as a Result of the Capitol Riot?" *FactCheck.org*, Mar. 21, 2022, factcheck.org/2021/11/how-many-died-as-a-result-of-capitol-riot. See also "24 Months Since the January 6 Attack on the Capitol," *United States Justice Department*, Jan. 4, 2023, justice.gov/usao-dc/24-months-january-6-attack-capitol#:~:text=Friday%2C%20January-ary%206%2C%202023%2C%20will%20mark%2024%20months,the%20process%20of%20affirming%20the%20presidential%20election%20results.

24. As Miller puts it: We butcher animals. We don't butcher people. (Miller, *Conflict Communication*, 18).

25. George Orwell, *1984* (New York: Signet, 1977), 9–16.

26. As an example from the psychological field, see Dolf Zillman and Jennings Bryant, "Pornography's Impact on Sexual Satisfaction," *Journal of Applied Social Psychology* 18, no. 5 (1988): 438–453. For the man-o-sphere, note that being anti-pornography was a foundational emphasis for the Proud Boys: Ira Glass, "626: White Haze," Sept, 22, 2017, in *This American Life*, produced by WBEZ Chicago, podcast, thisamericanlife.org/626/white-haze.

27. For example: Anna Moore, "Why Sex Is Better In a Long-Term Relationship," *The Guardian*, July 23, 2016, theguardian.com/lifeandstyle/2016/jul/23/why-sex-is-better-in-a-long-term-relationship.

28. Tina Fey, *Bossypants* (New York: Back Bay, 2011), 14–15.

29. "Castration Effects," *Go Ask Alice!*, Columbia University, March 22, 2002, goaskalice.columbia.edu/answered-questions/castration-effects.

30. Gerald May, *Addiction and Grace* (New York: Harper Collins, 1988), 133–139.

31. Scot McKnight, *Sermon on the Mount*, The Story of God Bible Commentary (Grand Rapids: Zondervan, 2013), 113–114.

32. McKnight, *Sermon on the Mount*, 124.

33. McKnight, *Sermon on the Mount*, 127.

34. Dietrich Bonhoeffer, *The Cost of Discipleship* (New York: Simon and Schuster, 1959), 82–83.

35. Emma Colton, "'This is who they are': Portland protesters filmed burning Bibles and American flag amid violence in city," *Washington Examiner*, August 2, 2020, washingtonexaminer.com/news/this-is-who-they-are-portland-protesters-filmed-burning-bibles-and-american-flag-amid-violence-in-city.

36. Madison Dapcevich, "Did Portland Protesters Burn Bibles and American Flags?," *Snopes*, August 11, 2020, snopes.com/fact-check/portland-protesters-burn-bibles.

37. Jerry Newcombe, "The Attack on Christ in Modern America," *Townhall*, August 6, 2020, townhall.com/columnists/jerrynewcombe/2020/08/06/the-attack-on-christ-in-modern-america-n2573800.

38. Ilona Bray, "What Counts as Persecution When Applying for Asylum or Refugee Status," NOLO, 2021, nolo.com/legal-encyclopedia/what-counts-persecution-when-applying-asylum-refugee-status.html.

39. Daniel Chirot and Clark McCauley, *Why Not Kill Them All?* (Princeton, NJ: Princeton, 2010).

40. Newcombe, "Attack on Christ."

41. Todd Nettleton, "Imprisoned for Christ: Former Prisoners Brunson, Baumann Speak," Mar. 13, 2021, in *VOM Radio*, produced by The Voice of the Martyrs, vomradio.net/episodes/detail/imprisoned-for-christ-former-prisoners-brunson-baumann-speak.

42. McKnight, *Sermon on the Mount*, 144.

43. M. Scott Peck, *The Road Less Traveled* (New York: Simon and Schuster, 1978), 81.

44. Richard Wurmbrand, *Tortured for Christ* (London: Hodder & Stoughton, 1967), 59.

45. Aleksandr Solzhenitsyn, *The Gulag Archipelago, 1918–1956: An Experiment in Literary Investigation, V–VII*, translated by Thomas P. Whitney (New York: Harper & Row, 1976), 259.

46. Aleksandr Solzhenitsyn, *The Gulag Archipelago, 1918–1956: An Experiment in Literary Investigation, III–IV*, translated by Thomas P. Whitney (New York: Harper & Row, 1974), 518.

47. Solzhenitsyn, *The Gulag Archipelago, III–IV*, 310.

48. Solzhenitsyn, *The Gulag Archipelago, III–IV*, 310.

49. Solzhenitsyn, *The Gulag Archipelago, III–IV*, 624.

50. Solzhenitsyn, *The Gulag Archipelago, III–IV*, 626.

51. Peck, *The Different Drum*, 187–200.

52. For starters, check out anything by Richard Foster.

53. Phyllis Tickle, *The Divine Hours* (New York: Doubleday, 2000).

54. McKnight, *Sermon on the Mount*, 164.

55. Susan Neiman, *Evil in Modern Thought* (Princeton, NJ: Princeton, 2002), 322.

56. Hall L. Calhoun in Leslie G. Thomas, *The Sermon on the Mount* (Nashville: Gospel Advocate, 1958), 120.

57. Lewis, *Narnia*, 87.

58. Lysa TerKeurst, *Forgiving What You Can't Forget* (Nashville: Nelson, 2020), 45–47.

59. TerKeurst, *Forgiving*, 53.

60. Aleksandr Solzhenitsyn, *The Gulag Archipelago, 1918–1956: An Experiment in Literary Investigation, I–II*, translated by Thomas P. Whitney (New York: Harper & Row, 1974), 502.

61. Solzhenitsyn, *The Gulag Archipelago, I–II*, 515.

62. Solzhenitsyn, *The Gulag Archipelago, I–II*, 591.

63. Harbinger and Dzubak, "Brooks."

64. Not "vermin." James seems to pull from a tradition common to the sermon Matthew records here (similar themes occur throughout his letter), and in his version of this, he talks about metal corroding (James 5:2–3).

65. They are also almost certainly the "rewards" God grants in Matthew 6:1–18.

66. Ira Glass, "515: Good Guys," Jan. 10, 2014, in *This American Life*, produced by WBEZ Chicago, podcast, thisamericanlife.org/515/good-guys.

67. Indeed, Jesus is probably playing off of the concept, common in many cultures, of the covetous "evil eye" (Matthew 20:15).

68. Reinhold Niebuhr, *The Nature and Destiny of Man: Volume I: Human Nature* (Louisville: Westminster John Knox, 1996), 179–186.

69. Lewis, *Narnia*, 524.

70. Karl D. Lehman and Charlotte E. T. Lehman, "Judgment and Bitterness as Clutter that Hinders Prayer for Emotional Healing," November 21, 2009, Documents, kclehman.com/index.php, 3–4.

71. Dallas Willard, *The Divine Conspiracy* (San Francisco: Harper Collins, 1988), 224.

72. Charlotte Lehman, "On the Art of Being Relationally Angry, Or, 'I Have a Pet Tiger,'" 2016, Documents, kclehman.com/index.php, 4.

73. For a practical look at a church that actually does this, see Eddy Hall, "The High Grace High Truth Church," Winter 2014, *EFCA Today*, efcatoday.org/story/high-grace-high-truth-church.

74. Bonhoeffer, *The Cost of Discipleship*, 43–56.

75. A "culture war" can be defined as a conflict between social groups for the dominance of their values, beliefs, and practices. The only Christlike way to go about this, the only way that shows respect for others, is to work to win hearts and minds. Turning to legislation is a clear indicator that we failed in this, so we're resorting to coercion. Surely there are ways

for Christians to engage in politics beyond the "war" paradigm. The world needs Christians who are interested in conversation, not domination.

76. Peck, *Different Drum*, 13–15.

77. Thomas, *Sermon on the Mount*, 154.

78. Thomas Keating, *The Human Condition* (New York: Paulist, 1999), 8–9.

About the Author

Jeremy lives in central Illinois with his three amazing kids. He has a bachelor's and master's in theology, which are not super-useful in the retail job he's worked since 2006. His theological training will probably come in handy once the kids are grown and he runs off to do Bible translation somewhere.

www.ingramcontent.com/pod-product-compliance
Lightning Source LLC
Chambersburg PA
CBHW020152090426
42734CB00008B/798